Point Pleasant Beach
New Jersey

The Docks - A Photo Essay, Circa 1970

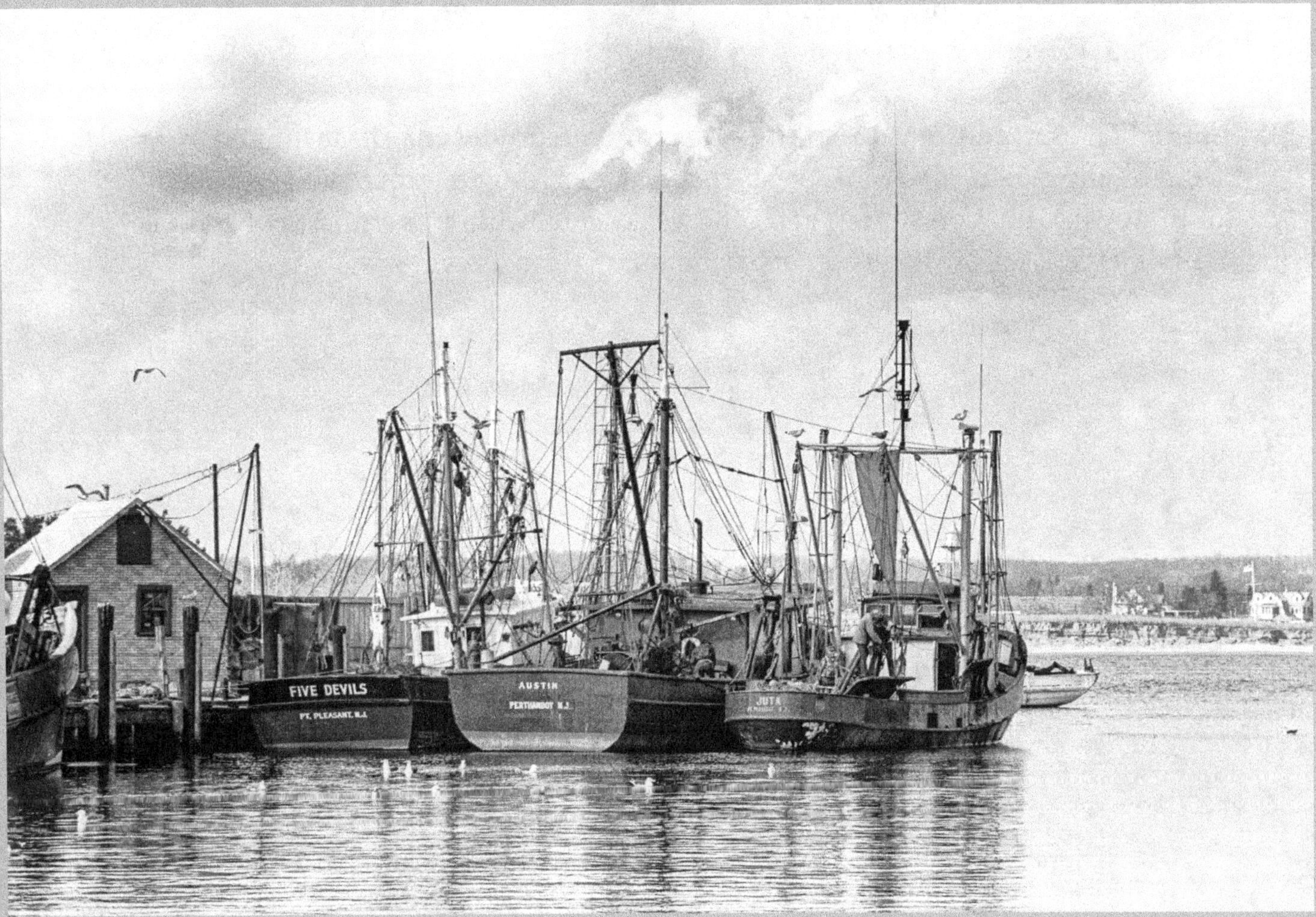

John Van Horn

johnvanhornphoto.net

Published by Moosic Mountain Wild Co.
Honesdale, Pennsylvania
www.moosicpublishing.com

ISBN: 1546984925
ISBN-13: 978-1546984924

All photographs by John Van Horn
Book and Cover Design by John Van Horn

Cover, Title Page and Below: Co-op Dock.

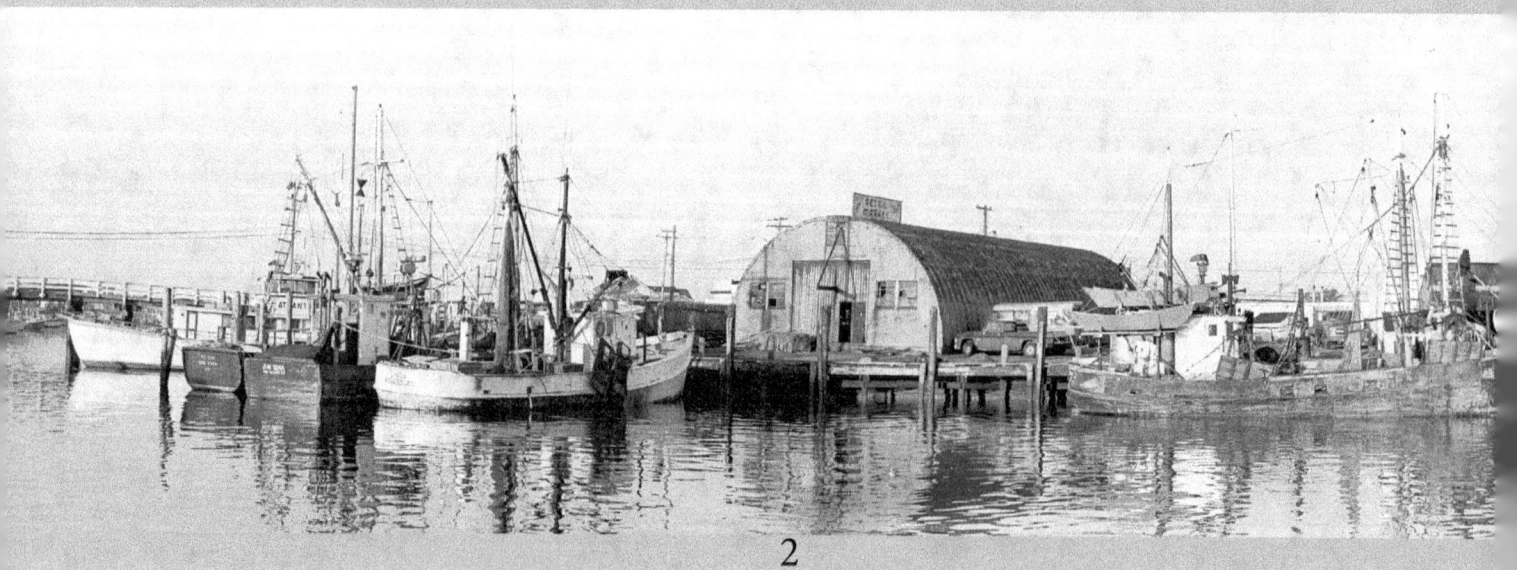

Introduction

From approximately 1968 to 1972 I photographed the commercial docks and fishing boats tied up to those docks in my hometown of Point Pleasant Beach, New Jersey. I was a college student who loved taking photographs and the subject matter was wonderful. Nearly fifty years later, the photos show a bygone era. Many of the commercial docks have survived, however, thanks to people with vision and commercial fishermen who are still committed to their profession.

This is a photo essay. At some juncture, I would like to write more complete captions if I can better identify the individuals, activities and boats in the photos.

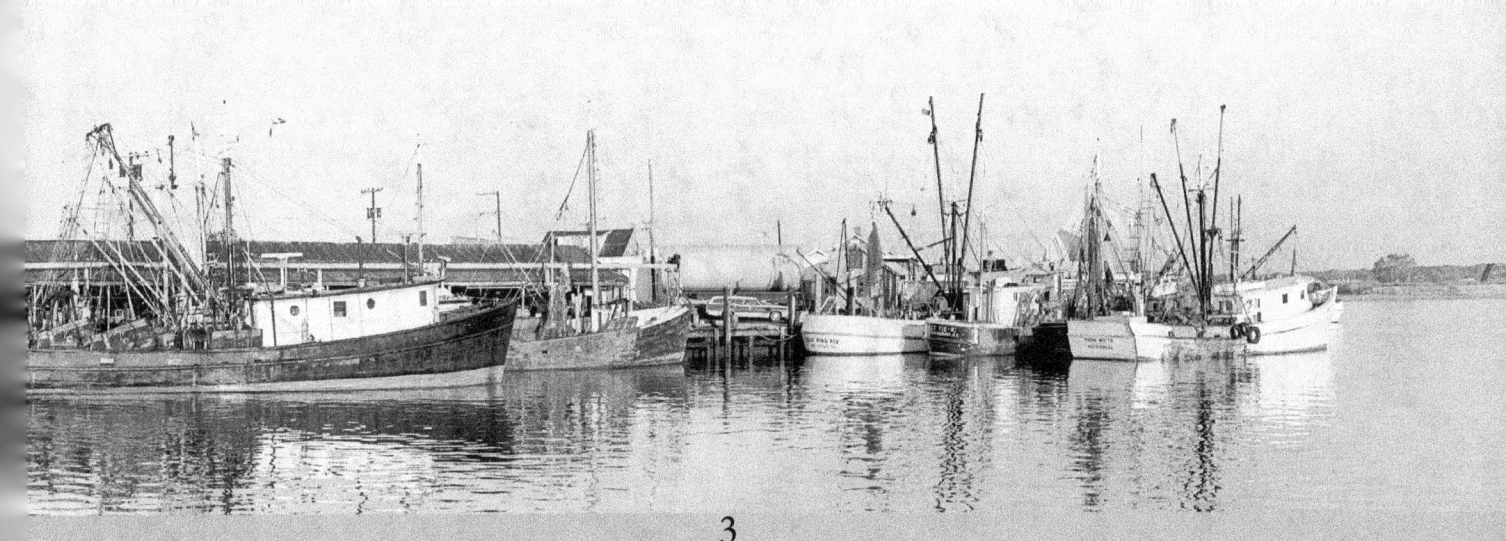

Looking up Cooks Creek with the Coast Guard Station on the left and the Co-op Dock on the right.

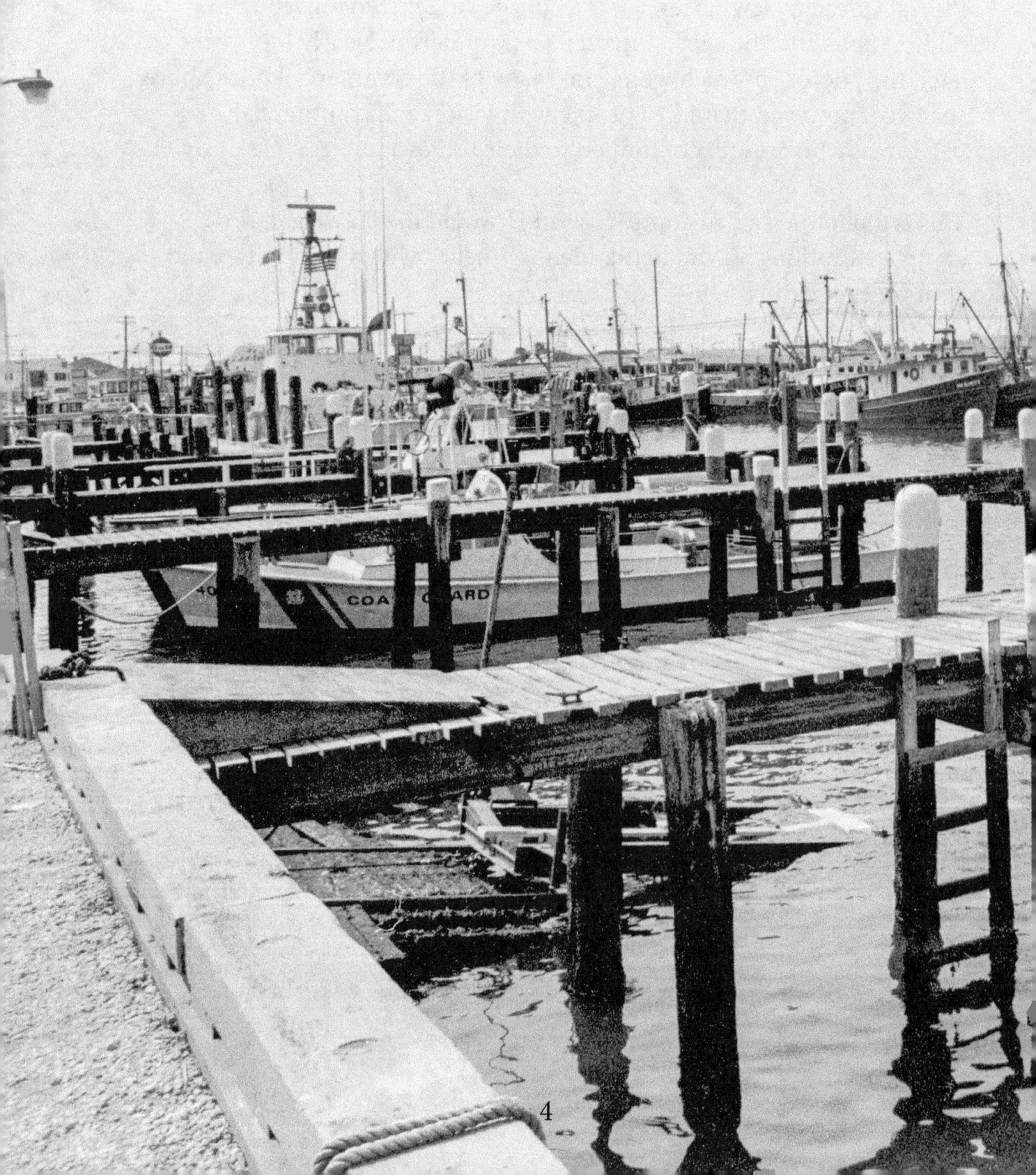

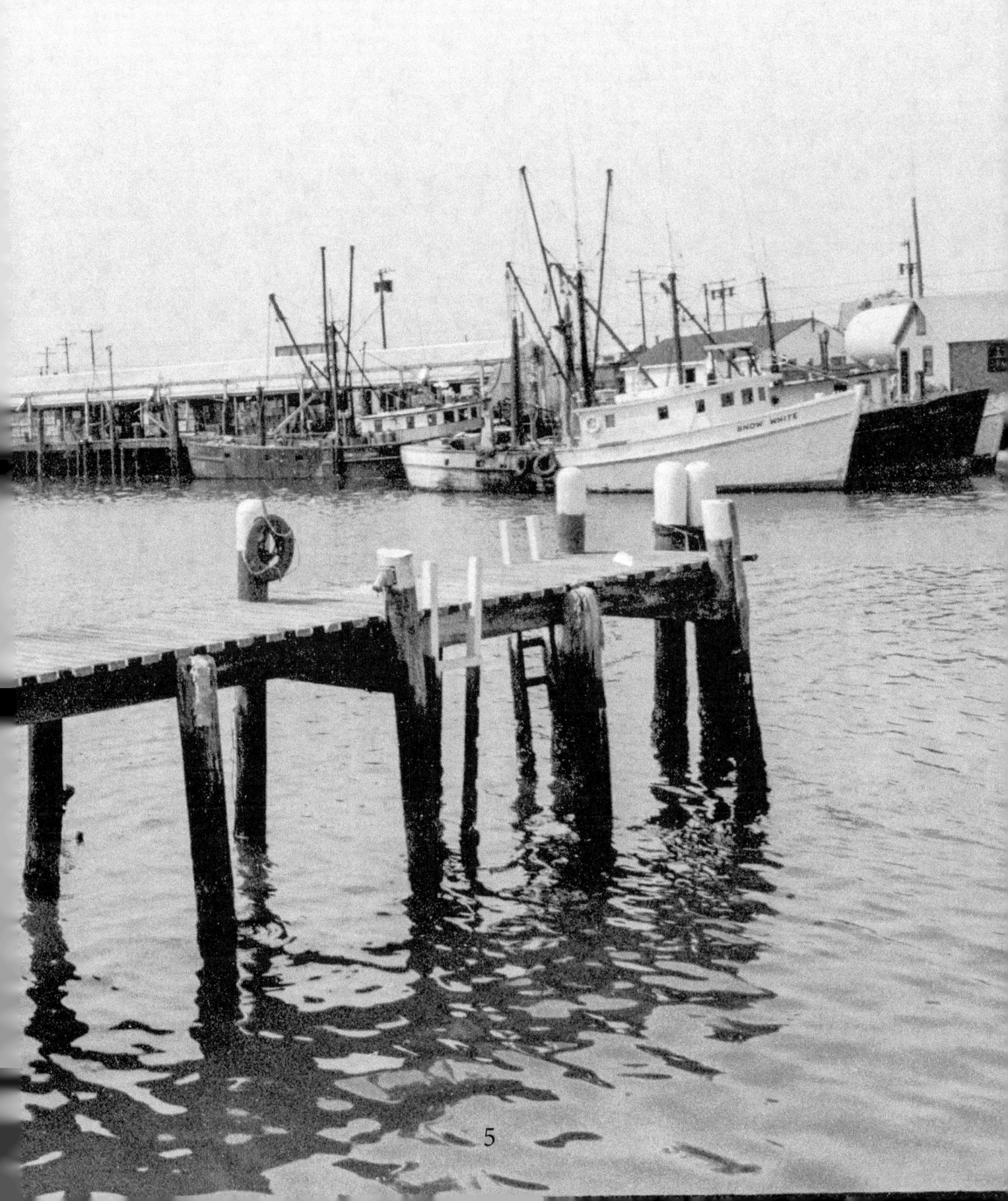

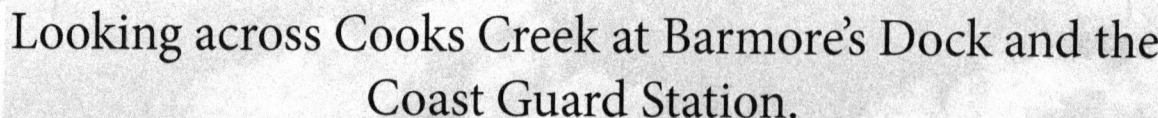

Looking across Cooks Creek at Barmore's Dock and the Coast Guard Station.

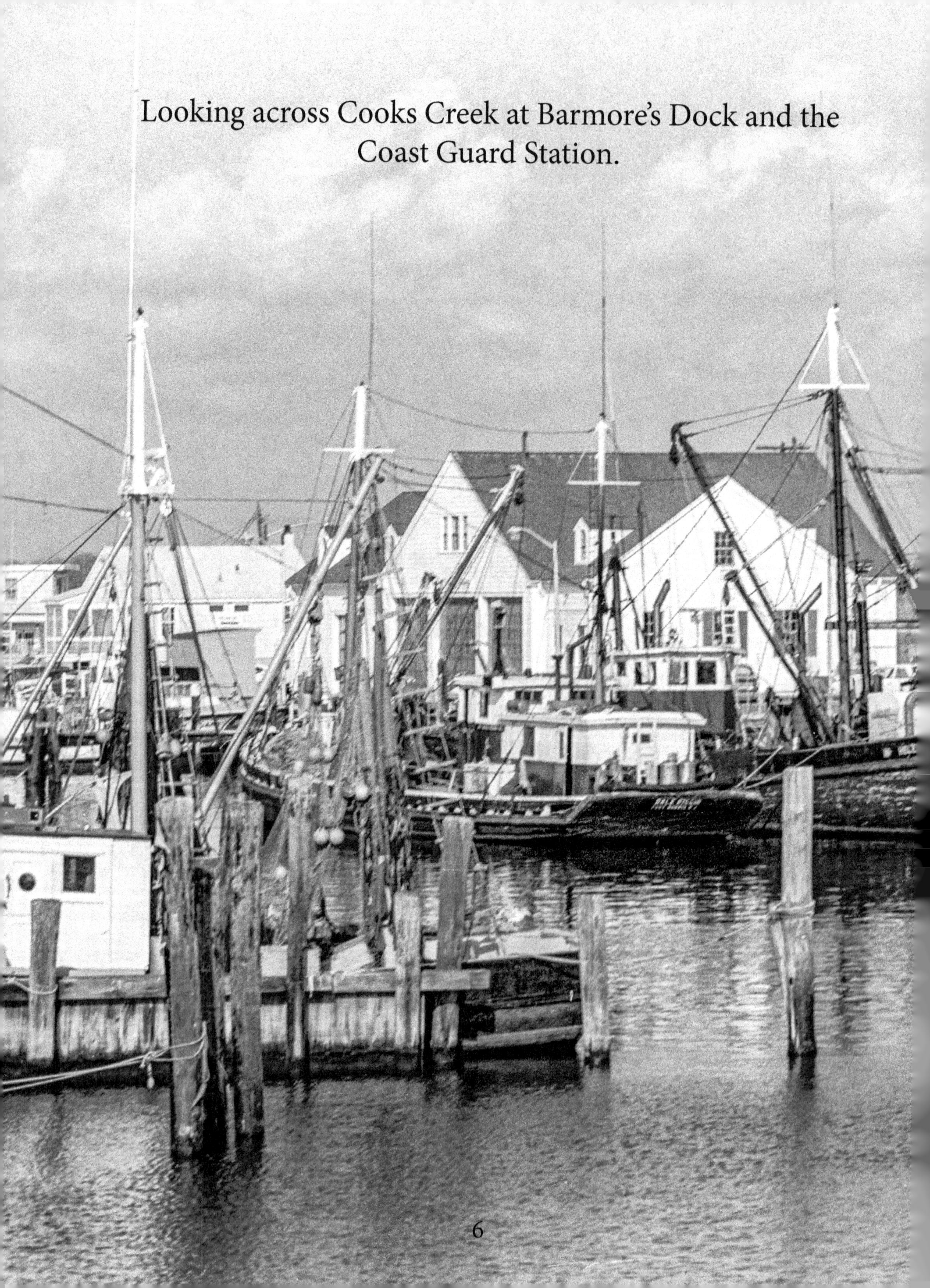

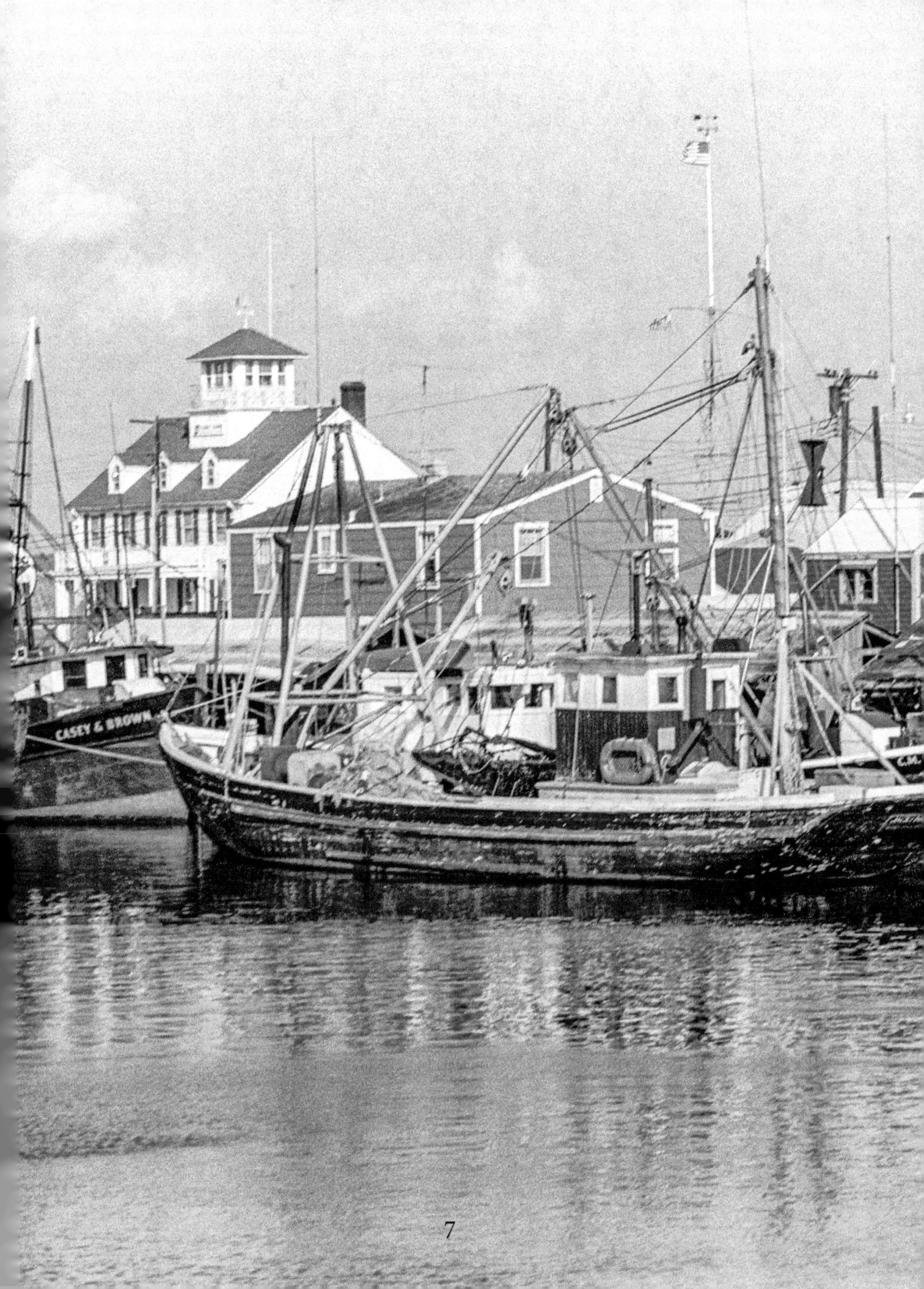

Barmore's Dock from across Cooks Creek.

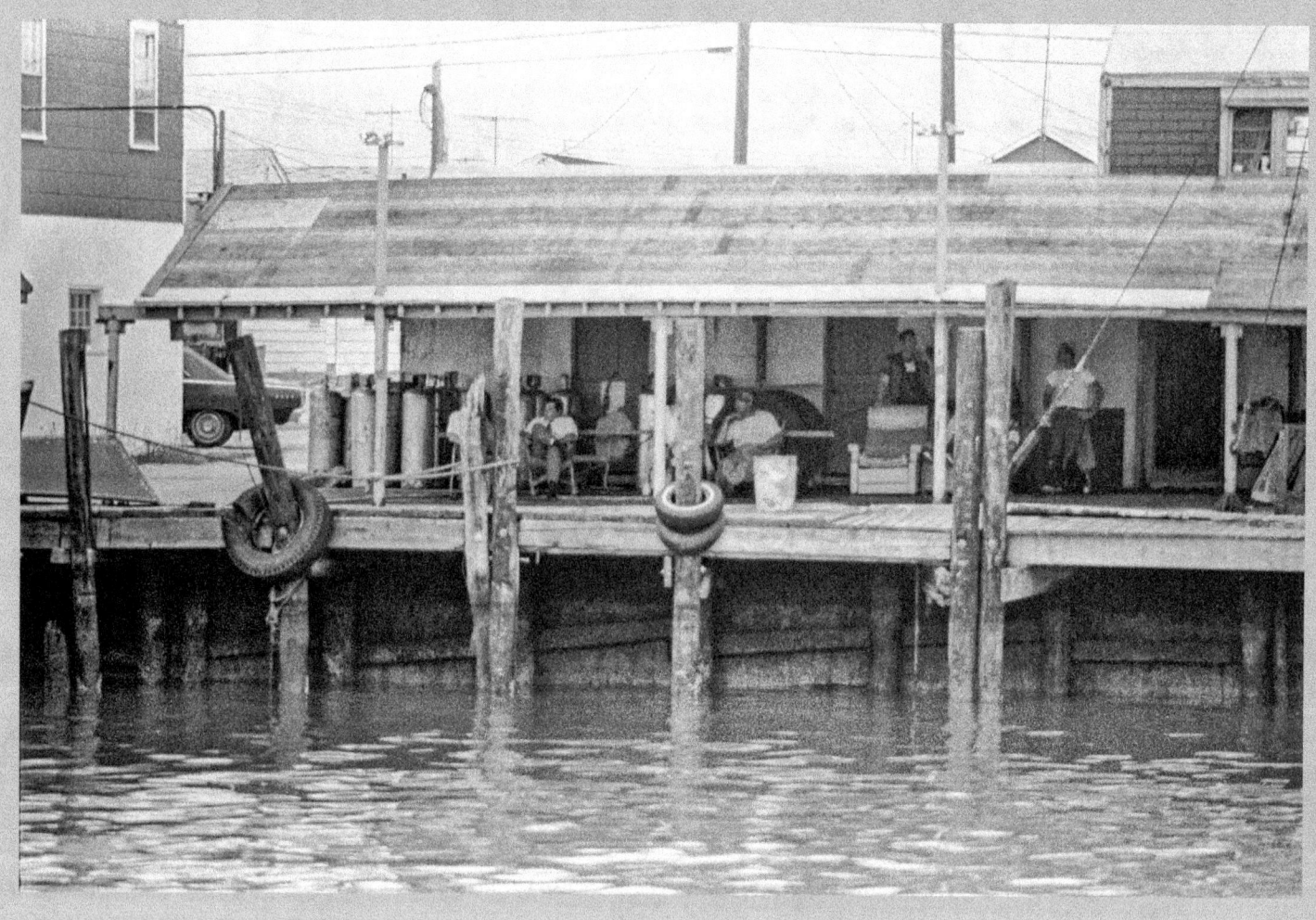

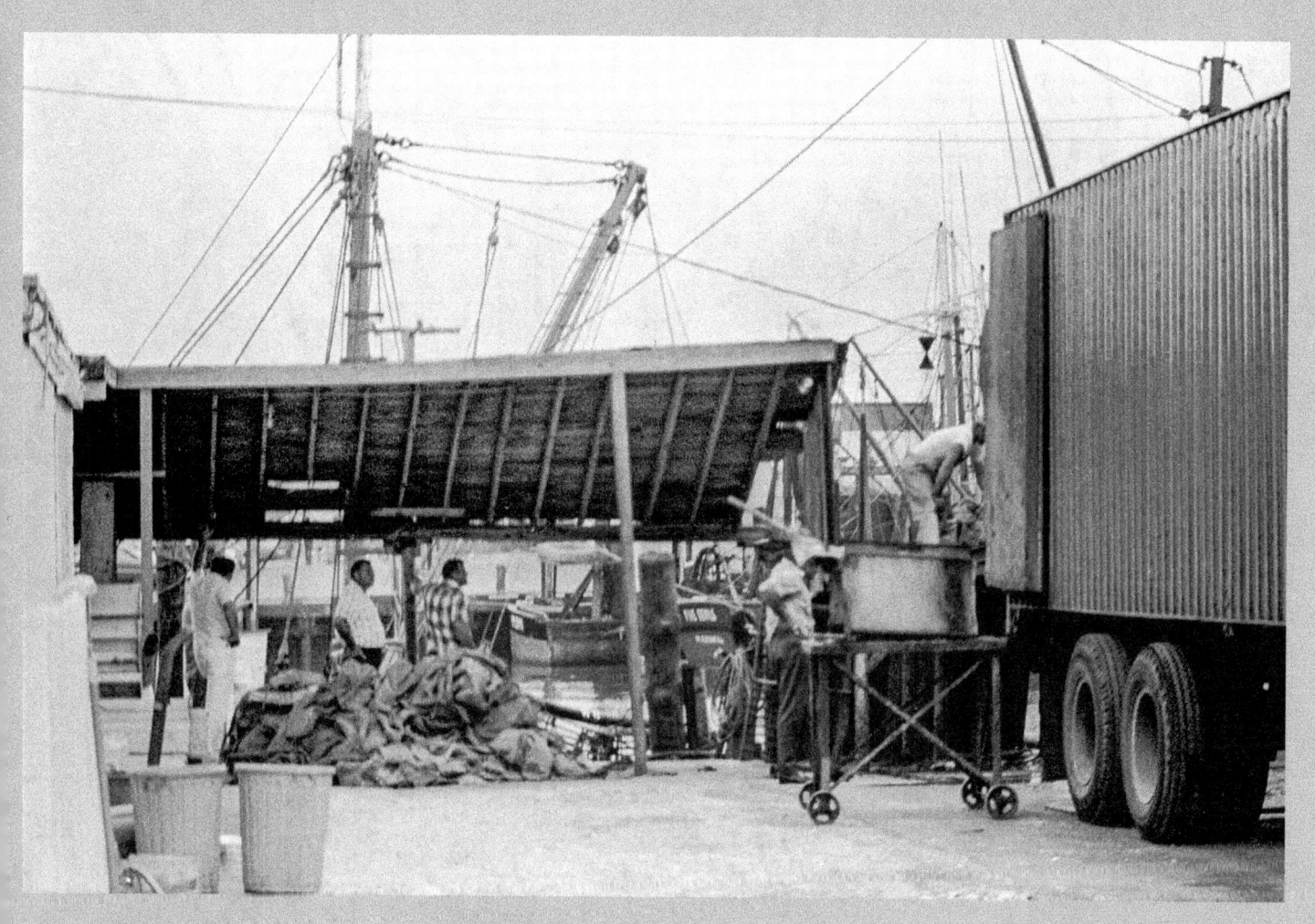

Barmore's Dock from Inlet Drive.

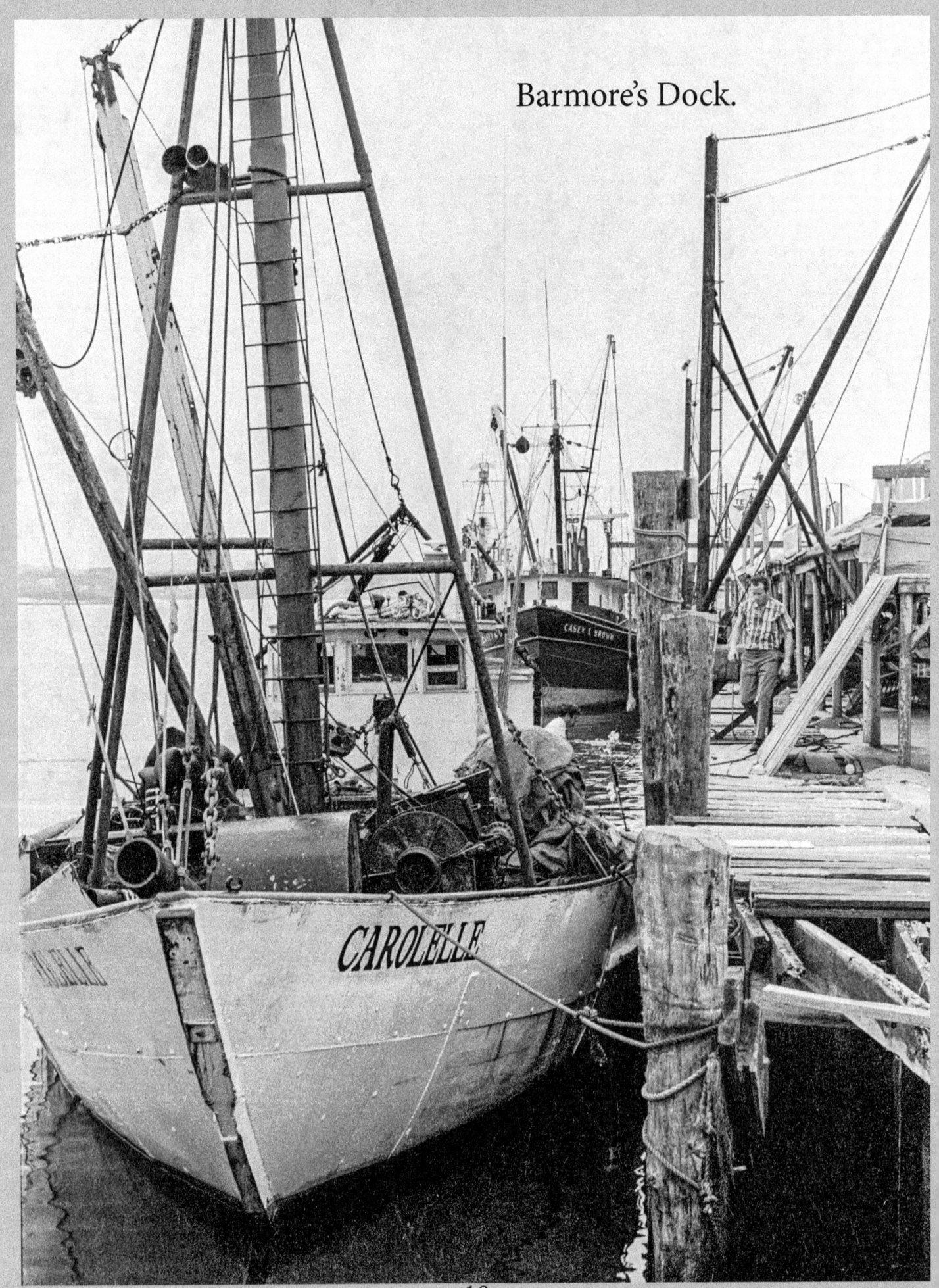

Barmore's Dock.

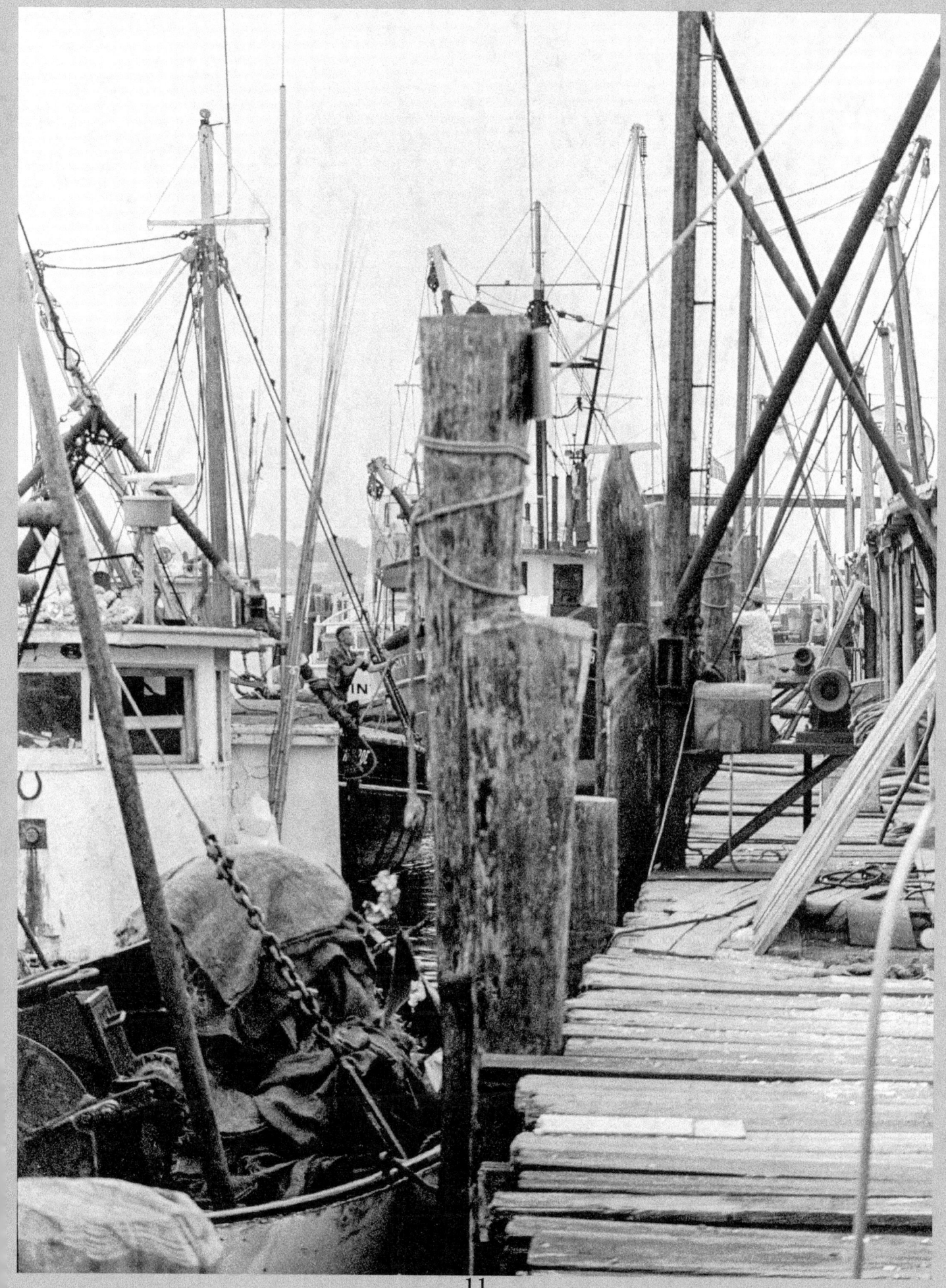

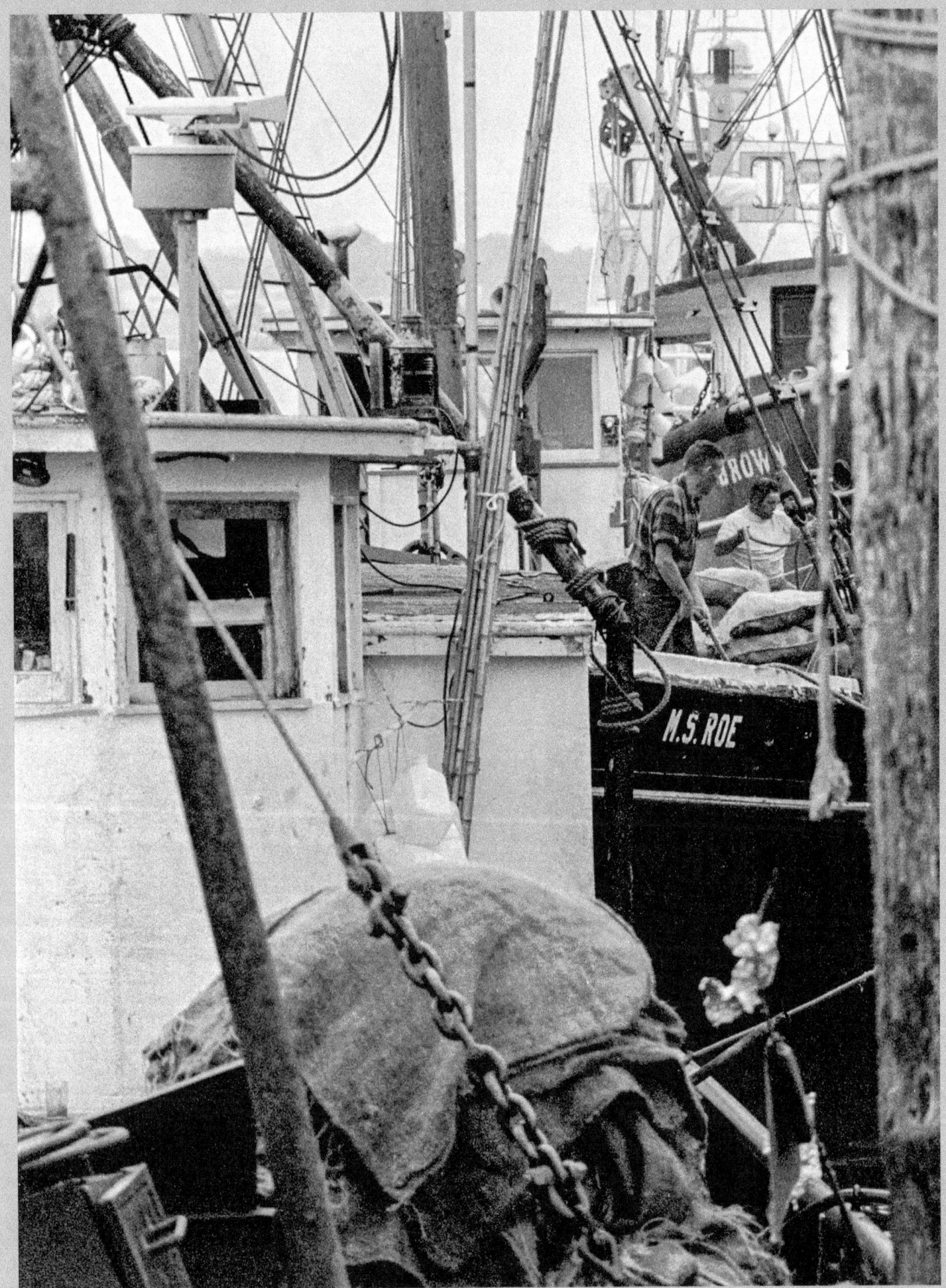

Looking down Cooks Creek from the Broadway Bridge. Barmore's Dock has been torn down and the Shrimp Box Restaurant has been expanded.

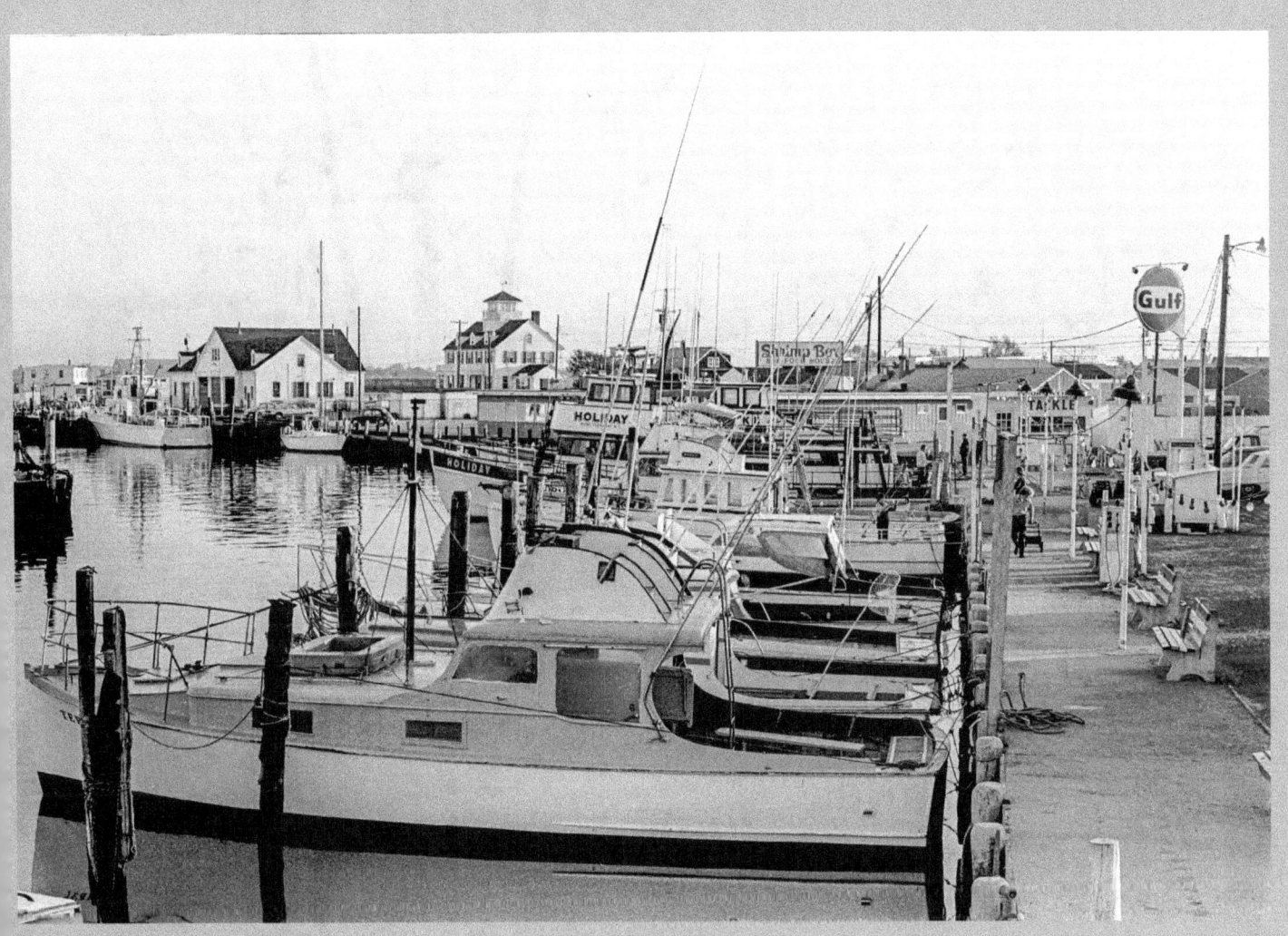

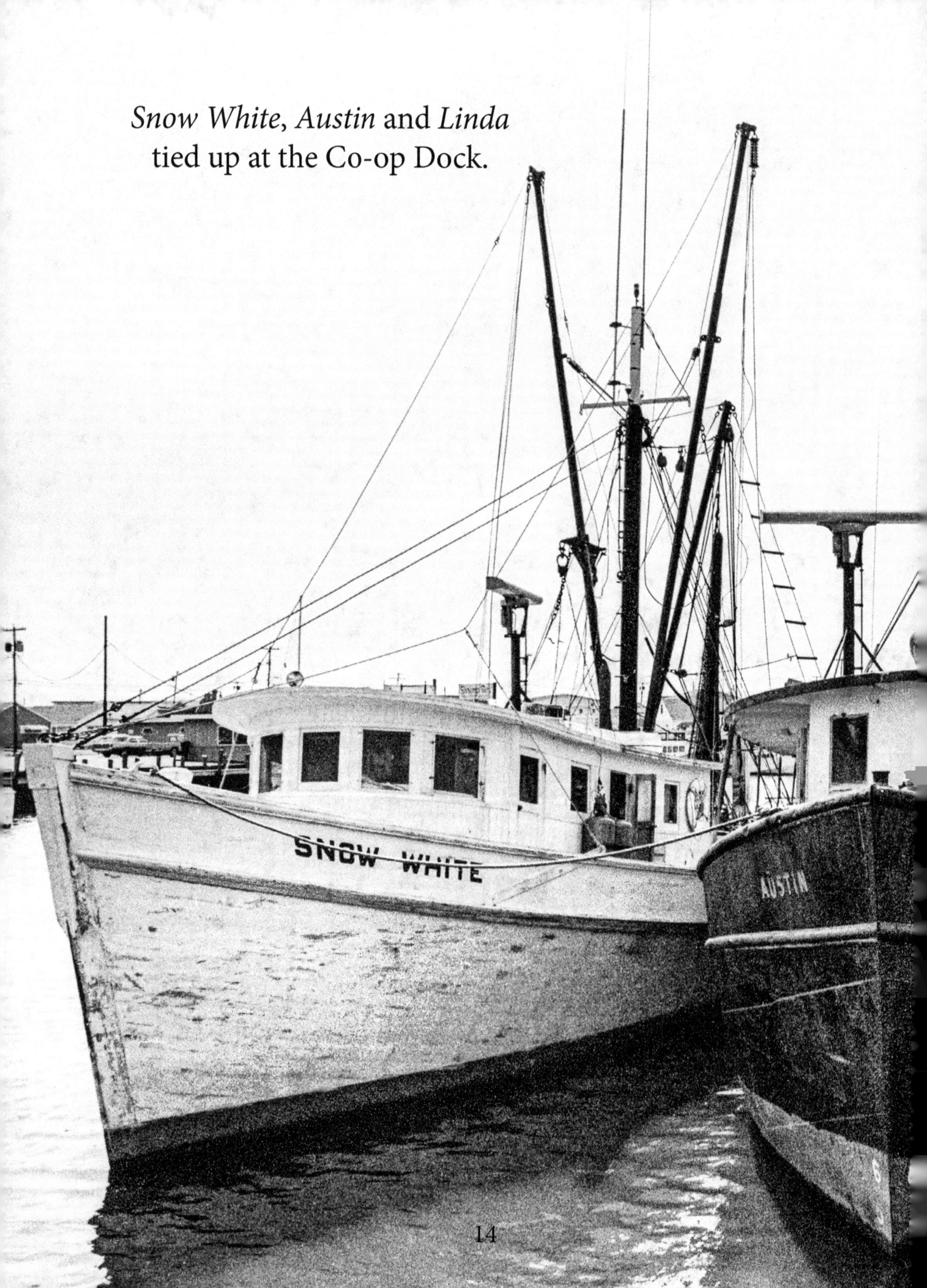

Snow White, Austin and *Linda* tied up at the Co-op Dock.

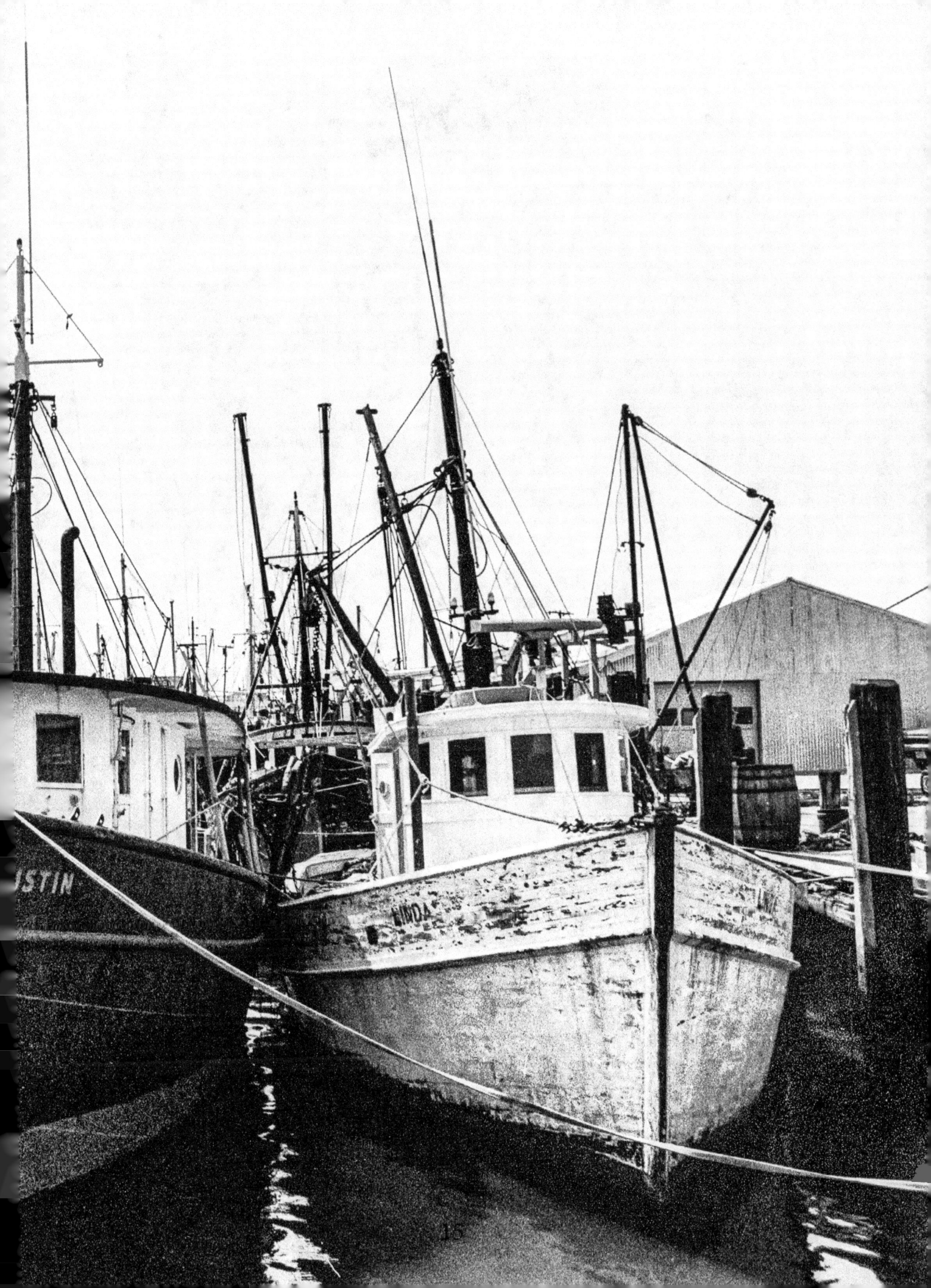

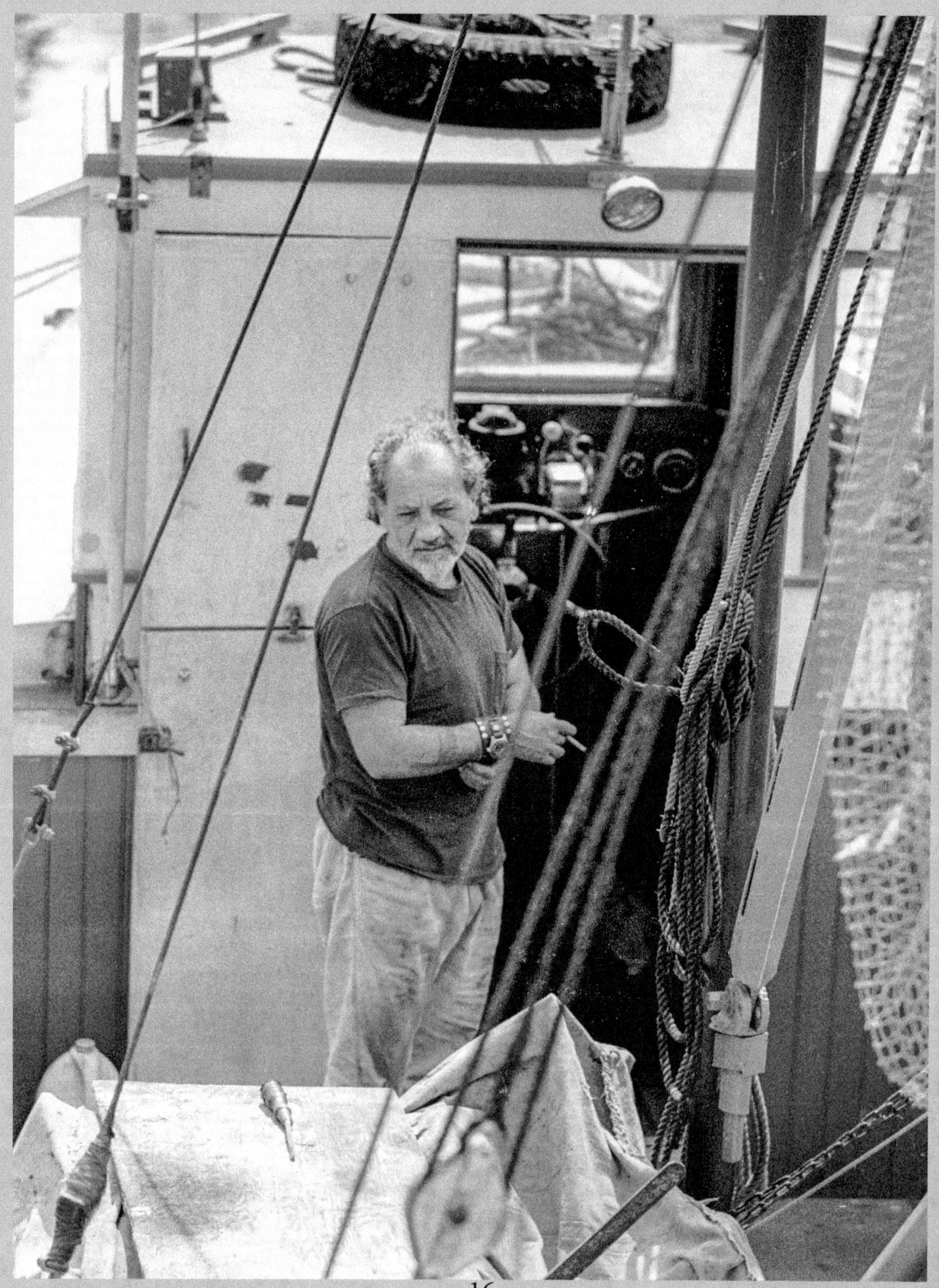

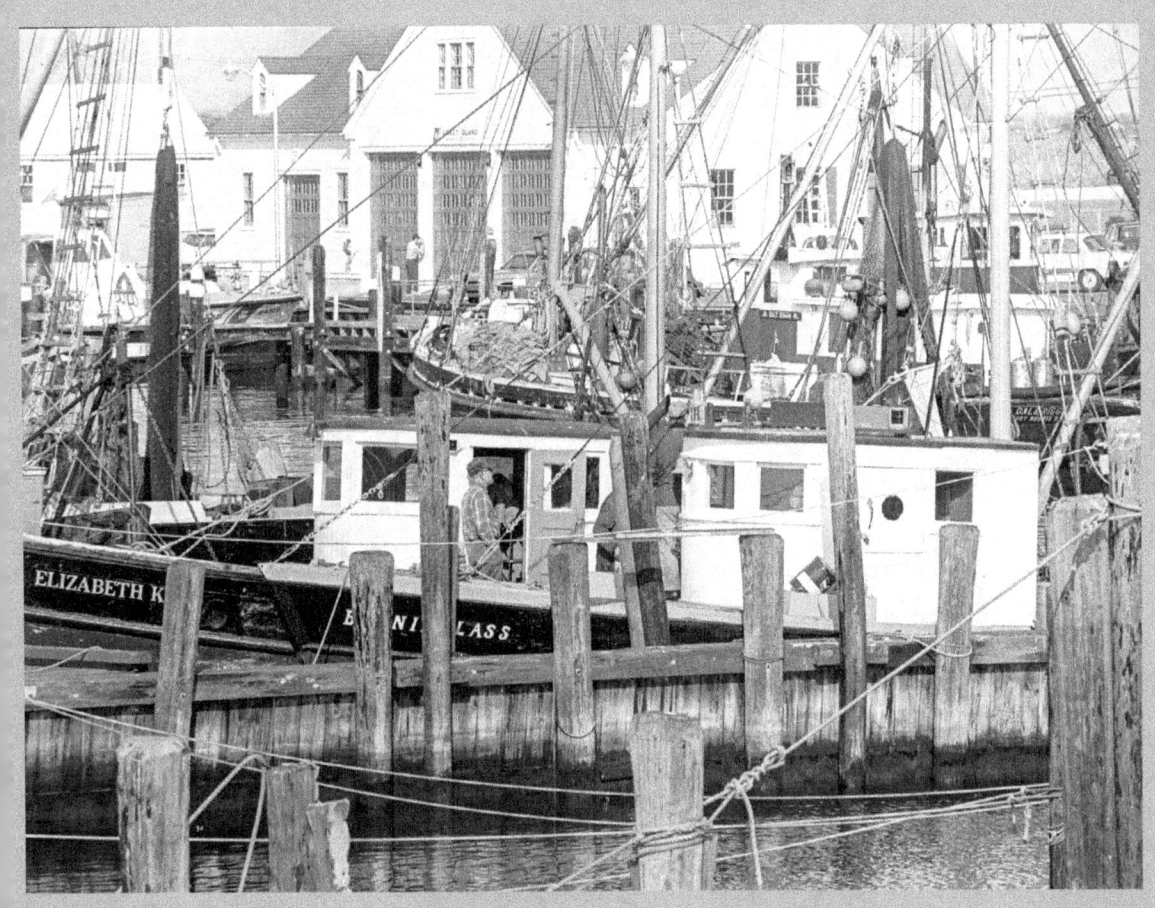

Boats at the Co-op Dock.

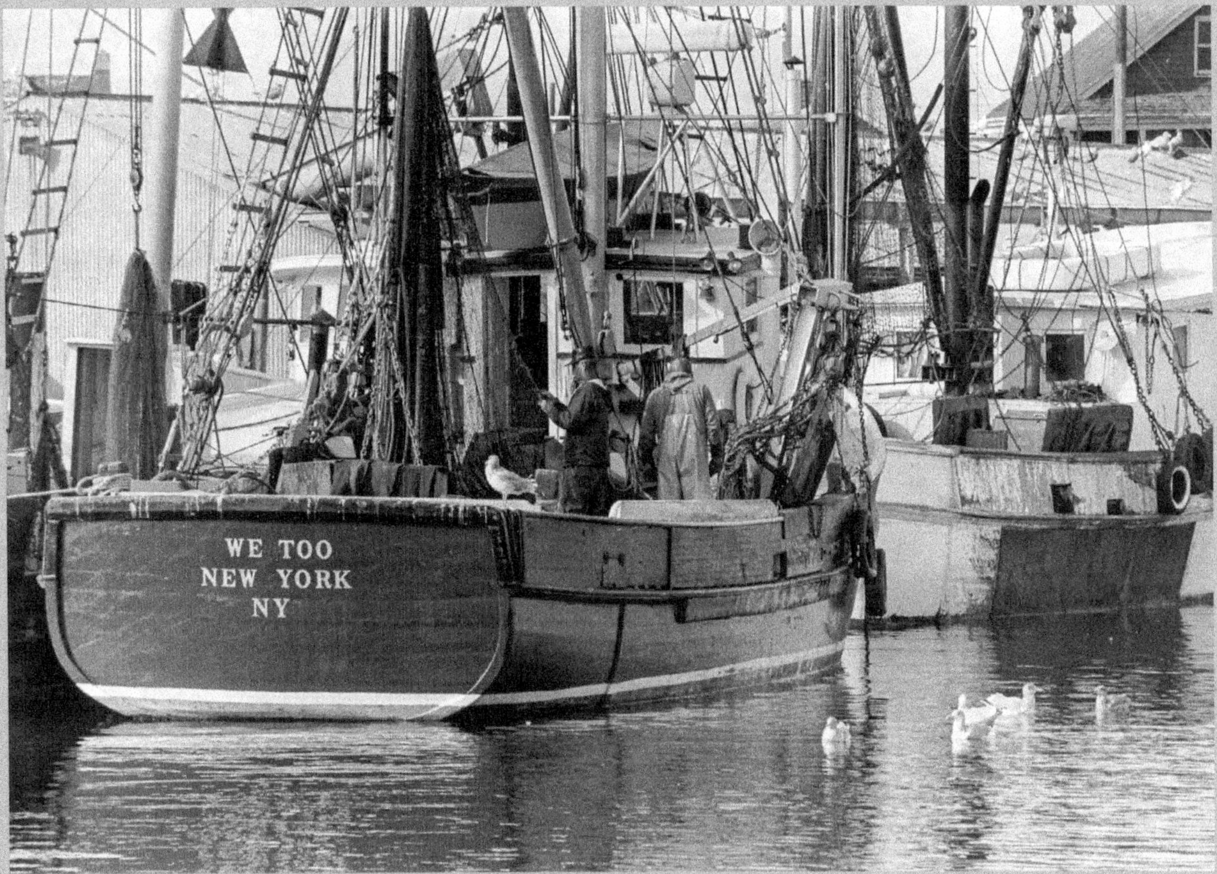

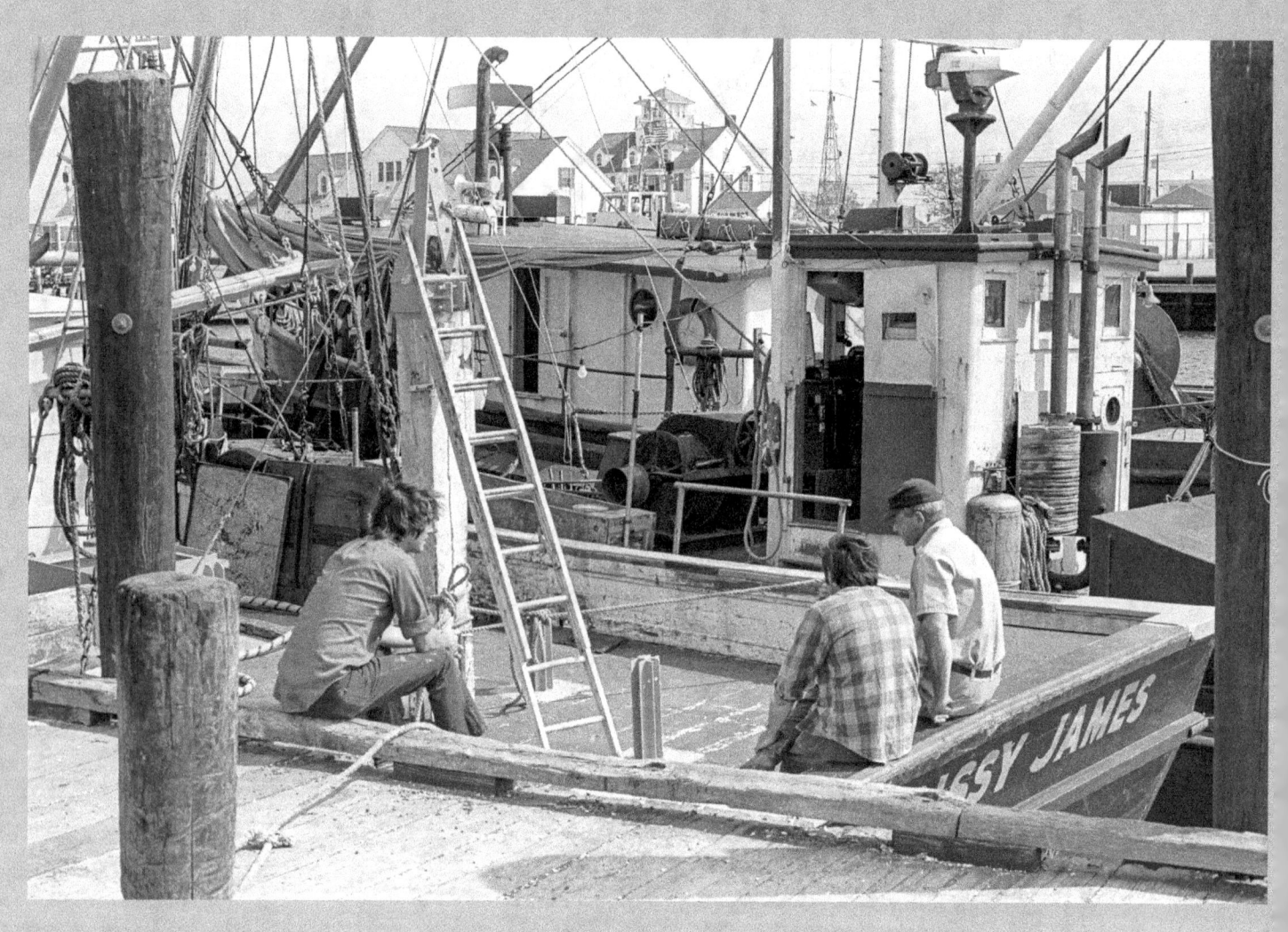

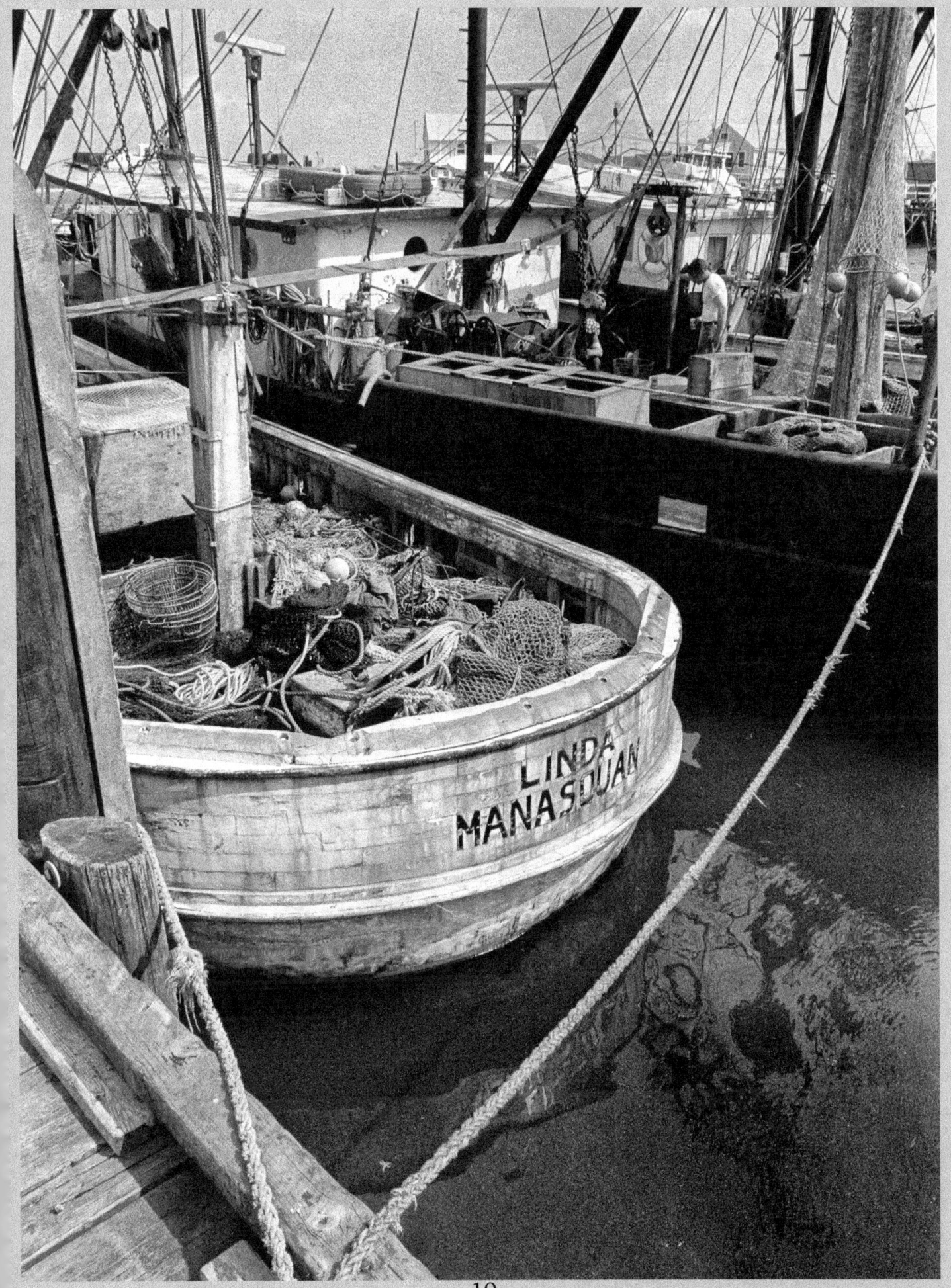

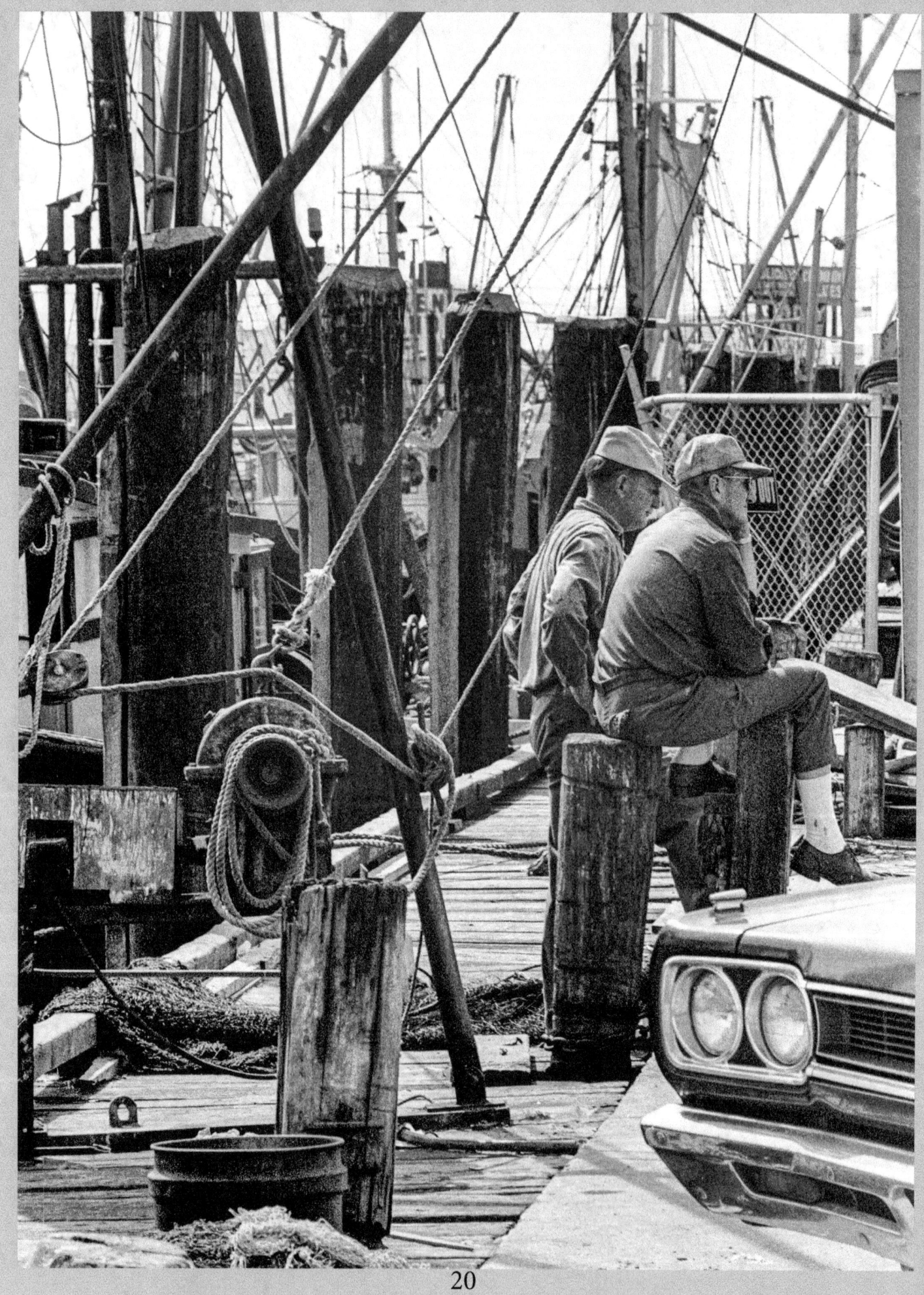

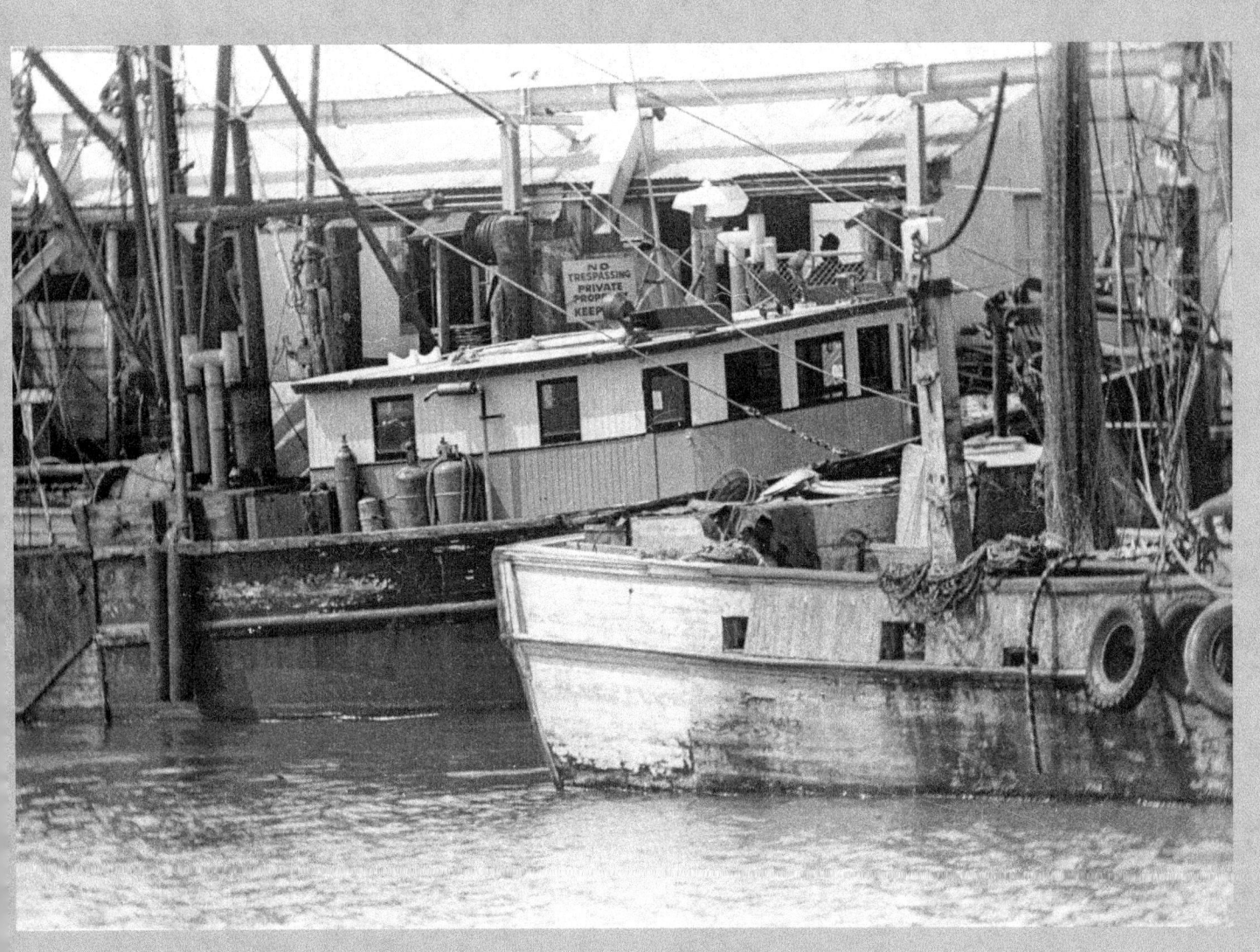

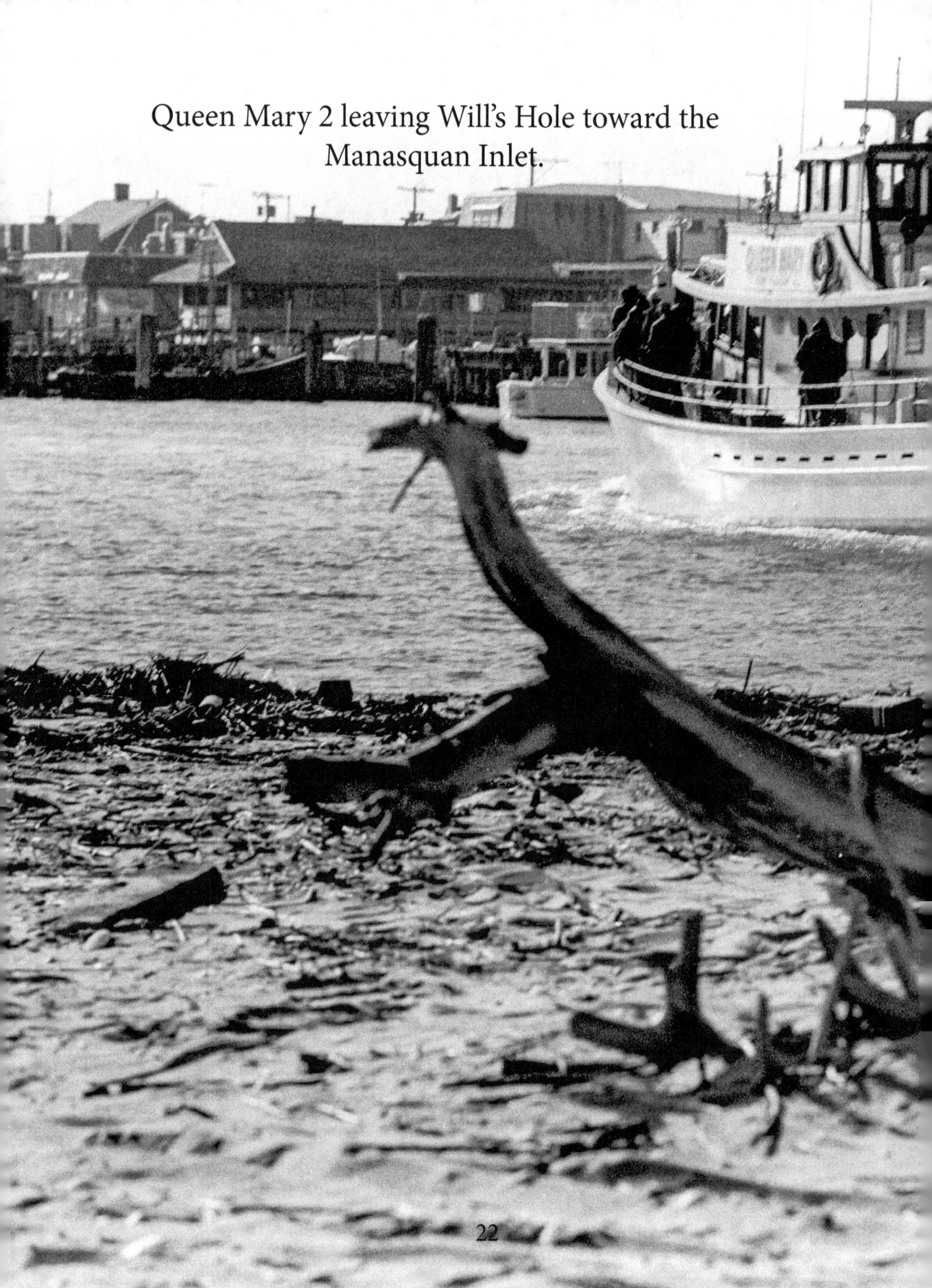

Queen Mary 2 leaving Will's Hole toward the Manasquan Inlet.

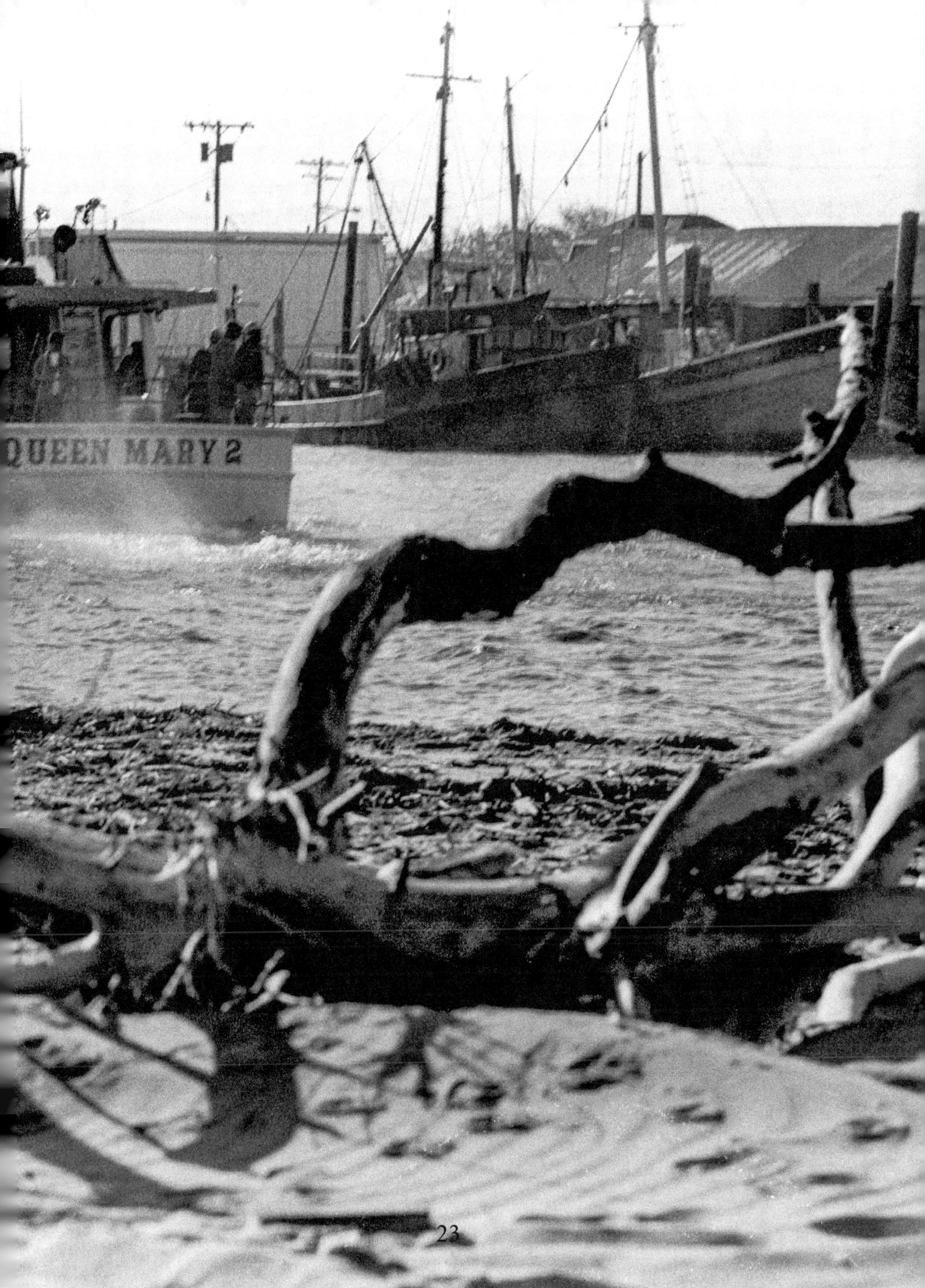

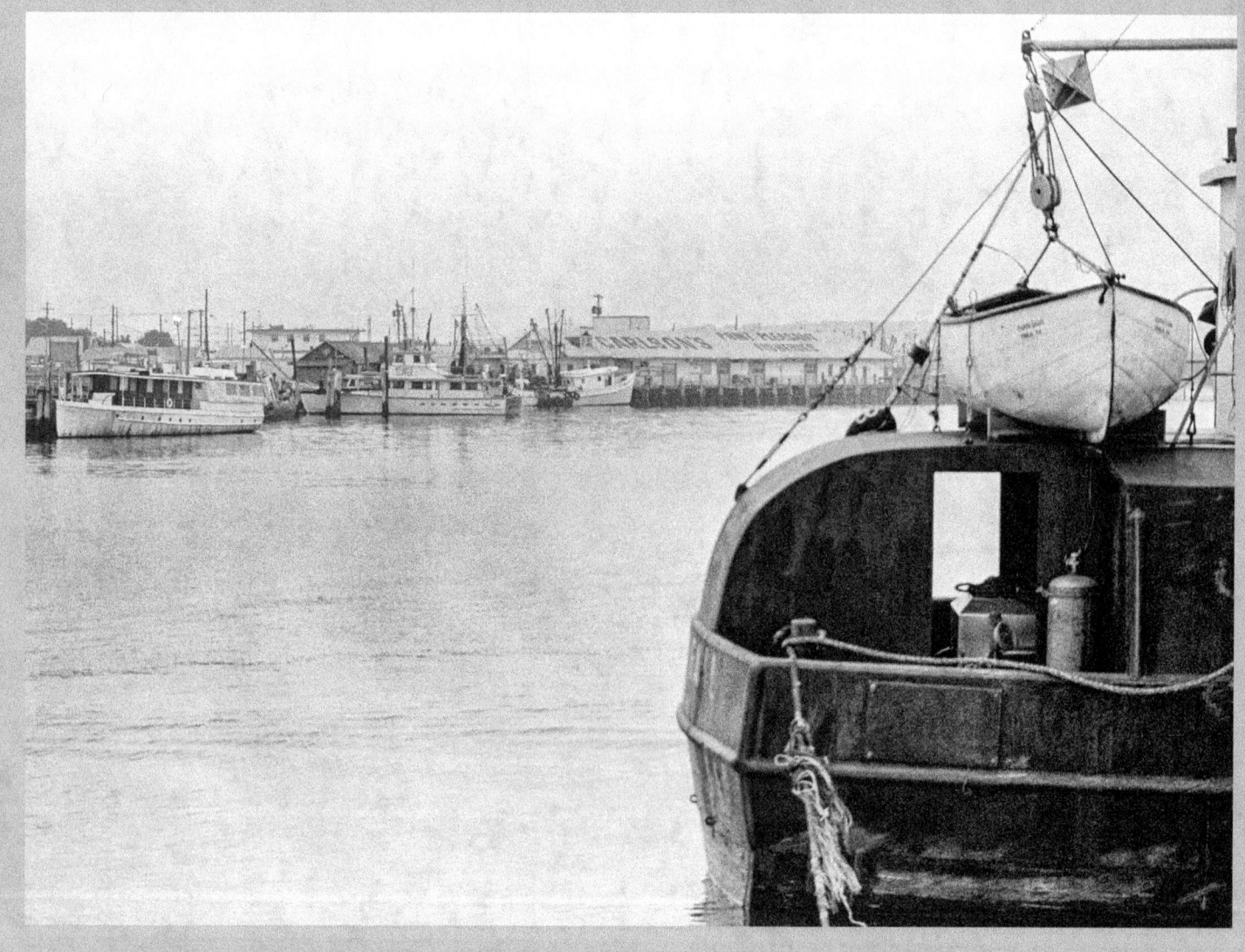

Above: Taken from Inlet Drive with Carlson's Fishery in the background.

Opposite: Looking into the morning sun from Carlson's Fishery.

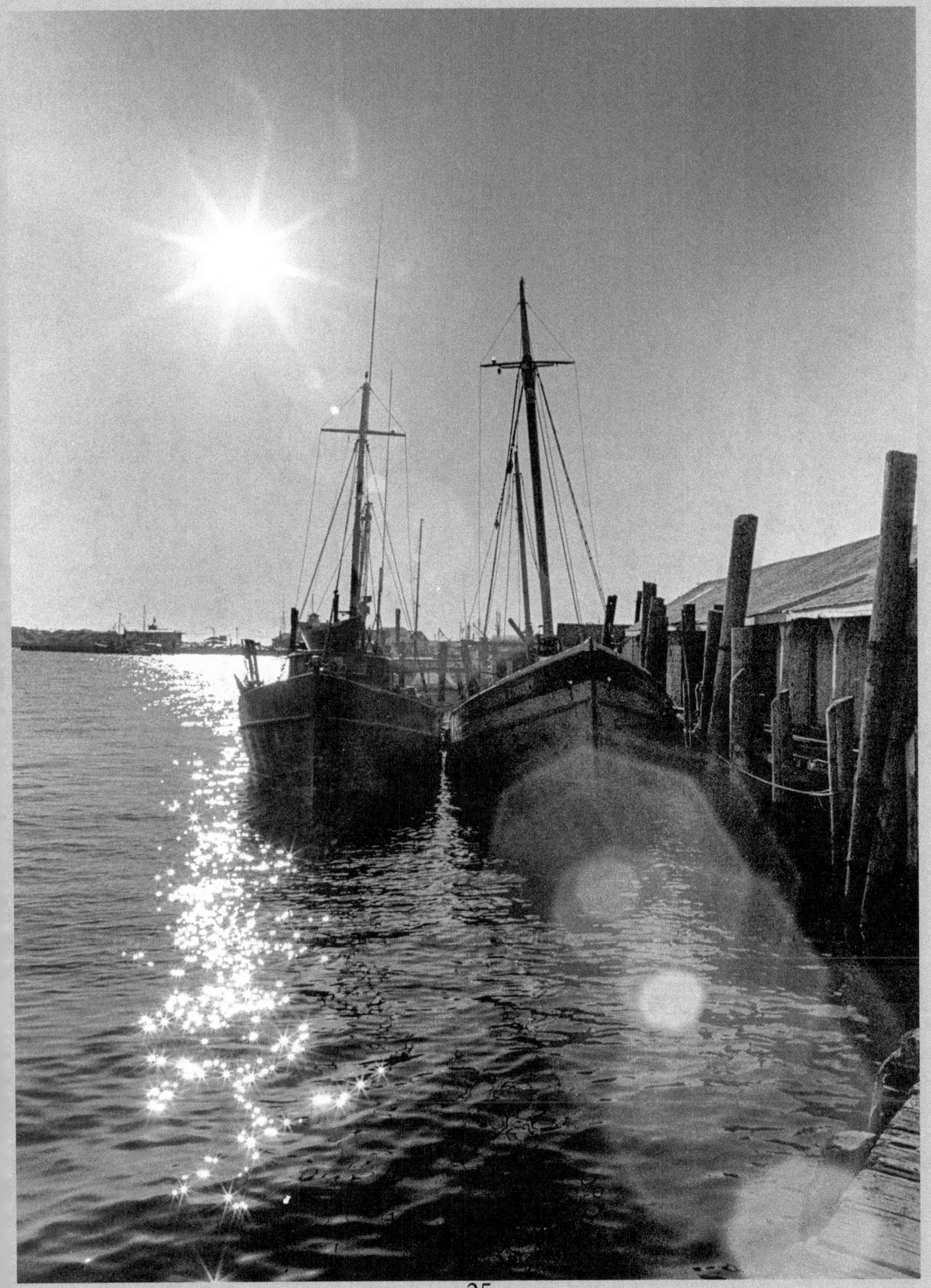

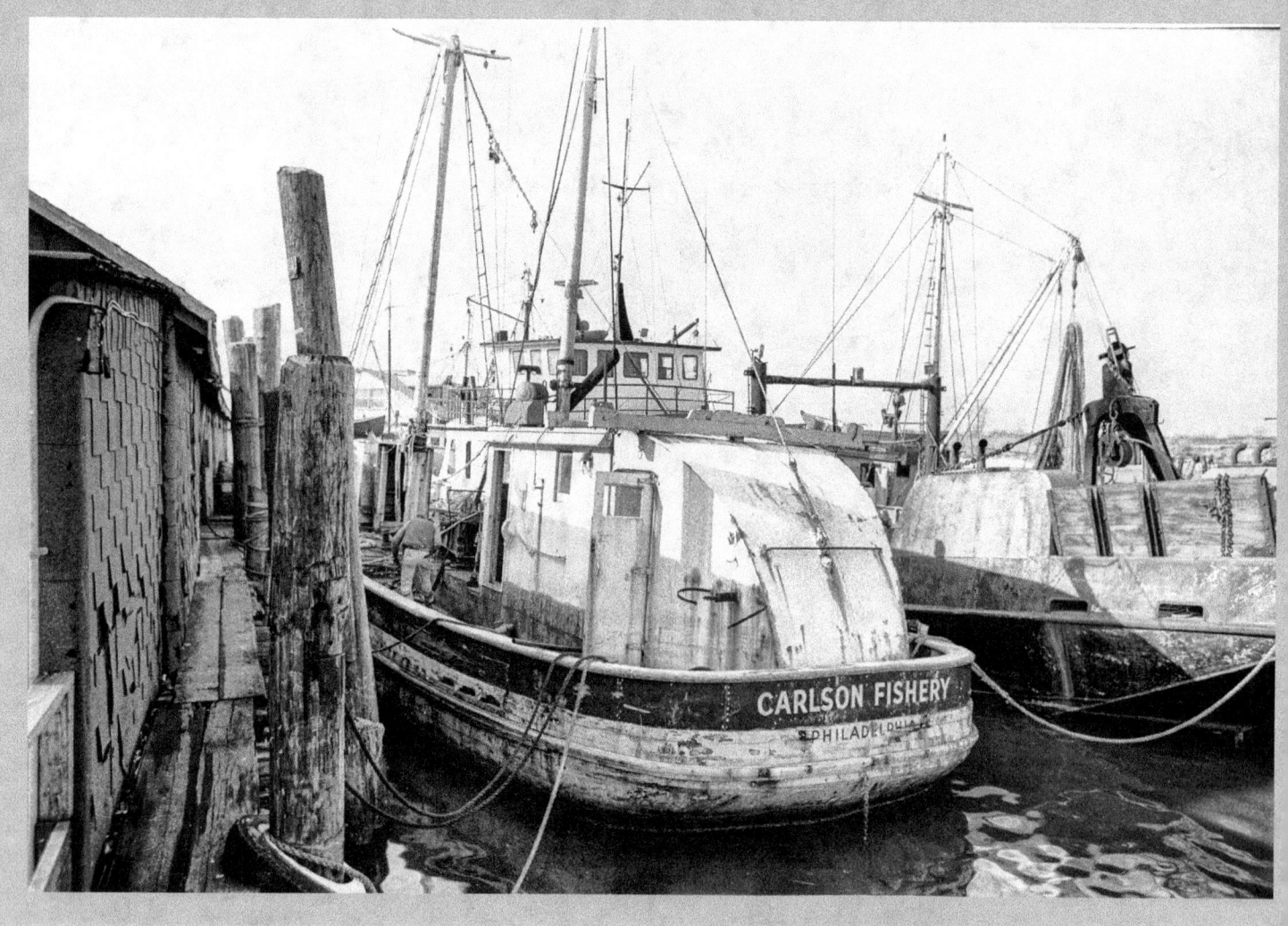

Above and Opposite: Photos of boats at Carlson's Fishery.

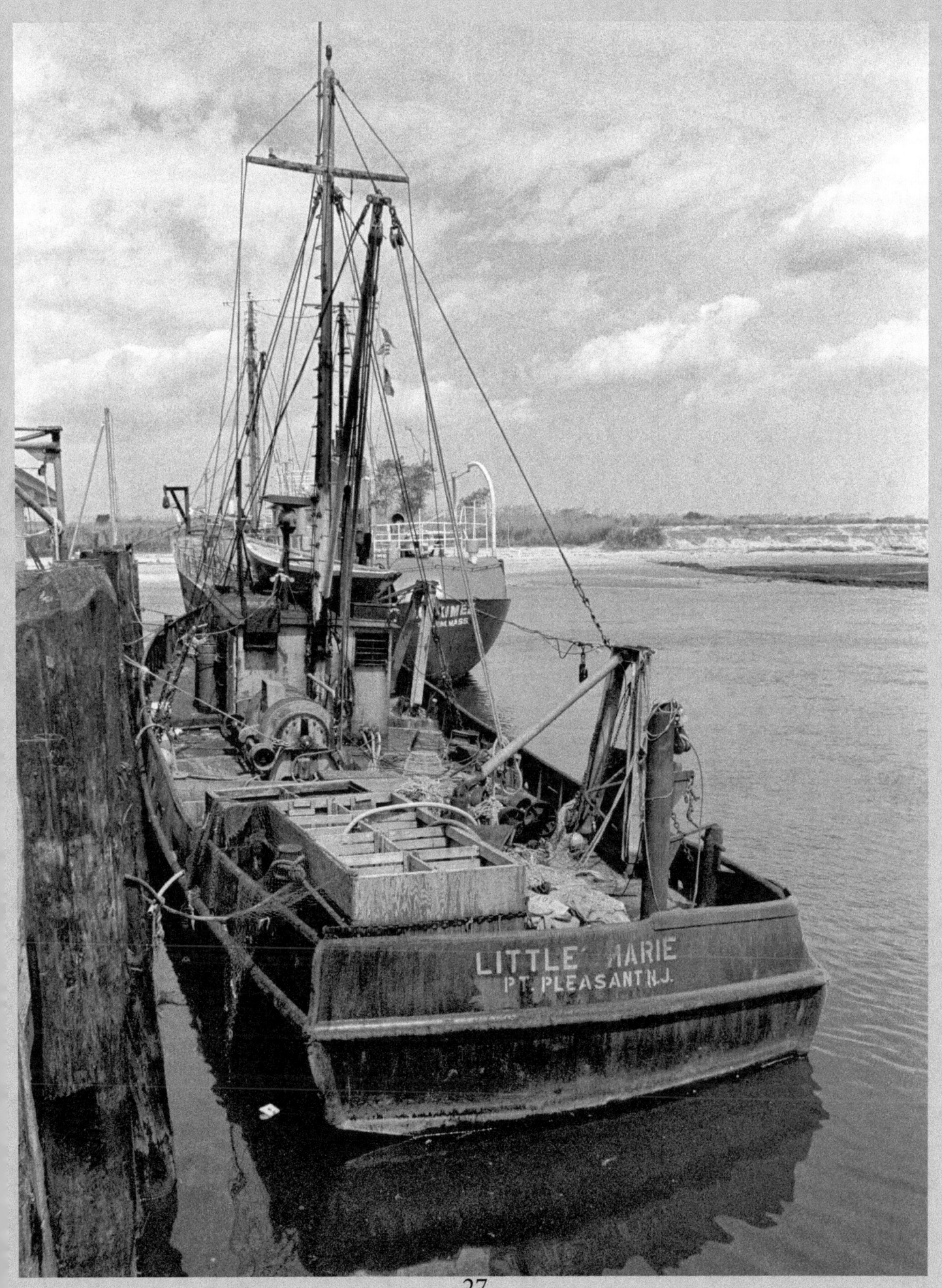

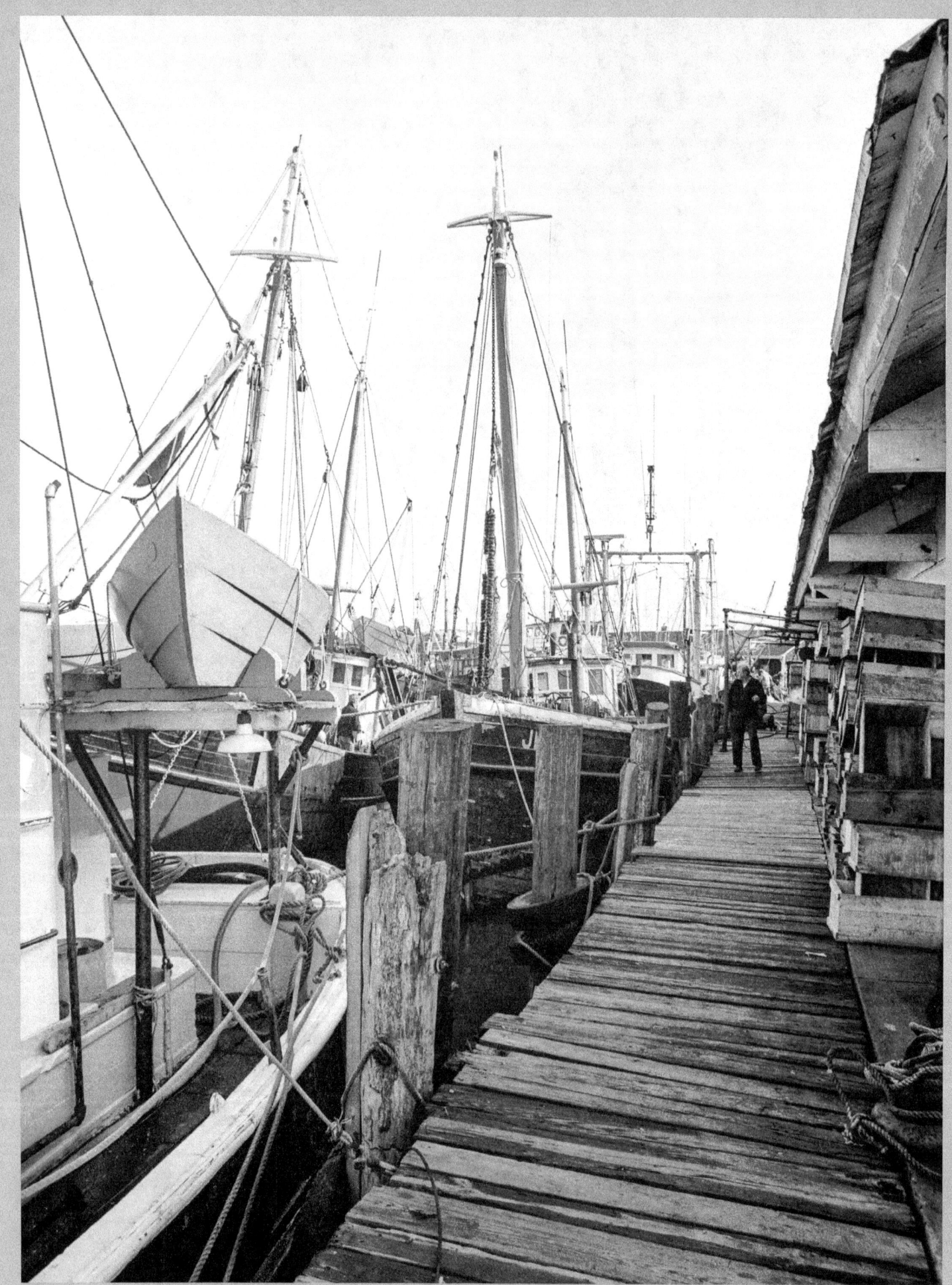

Opposite: On the dock of Carlson's Fishery.

Below: Looking west toward what I always called the "clam factory," now Atlantic Capes Fisheries.

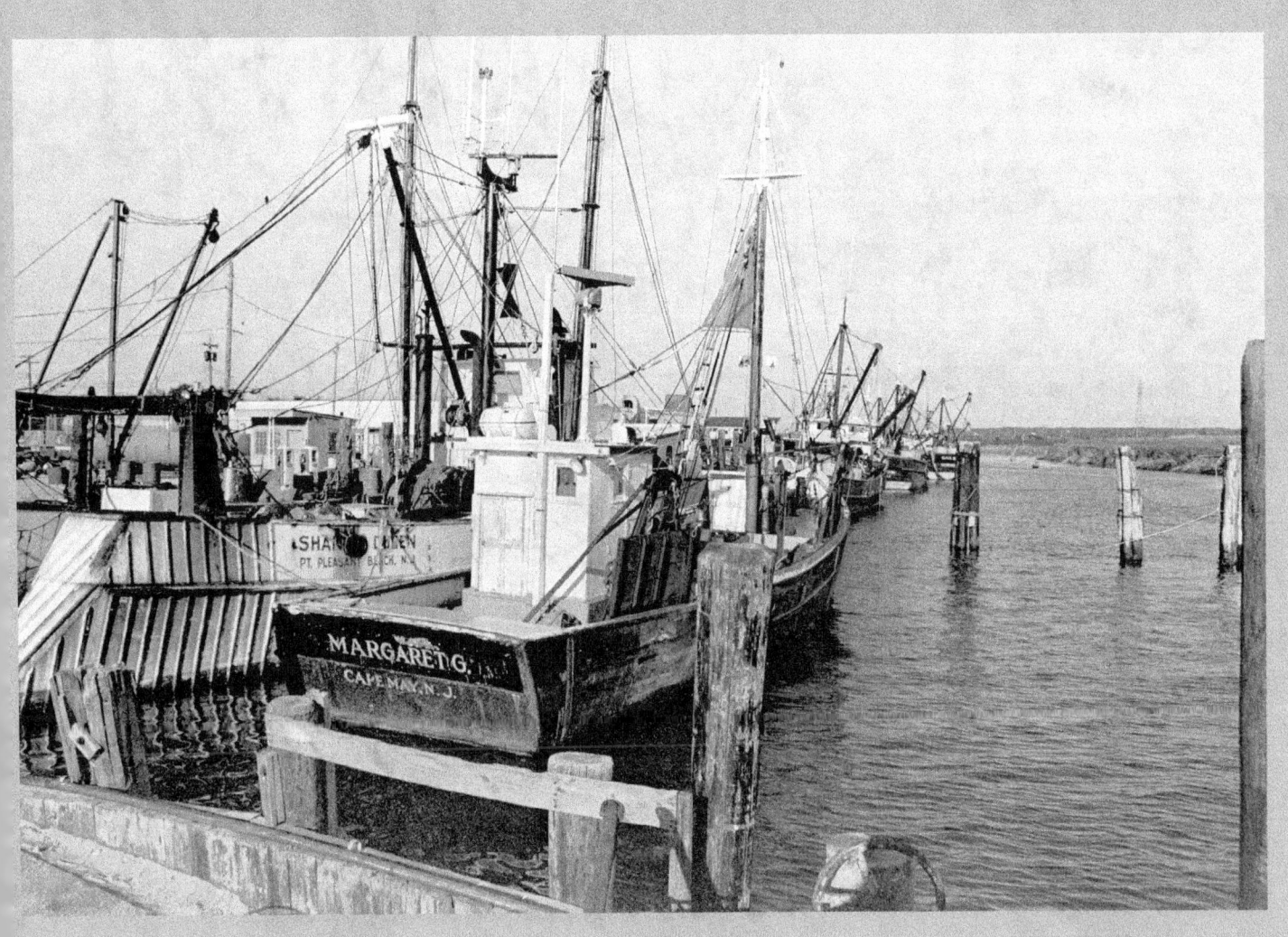

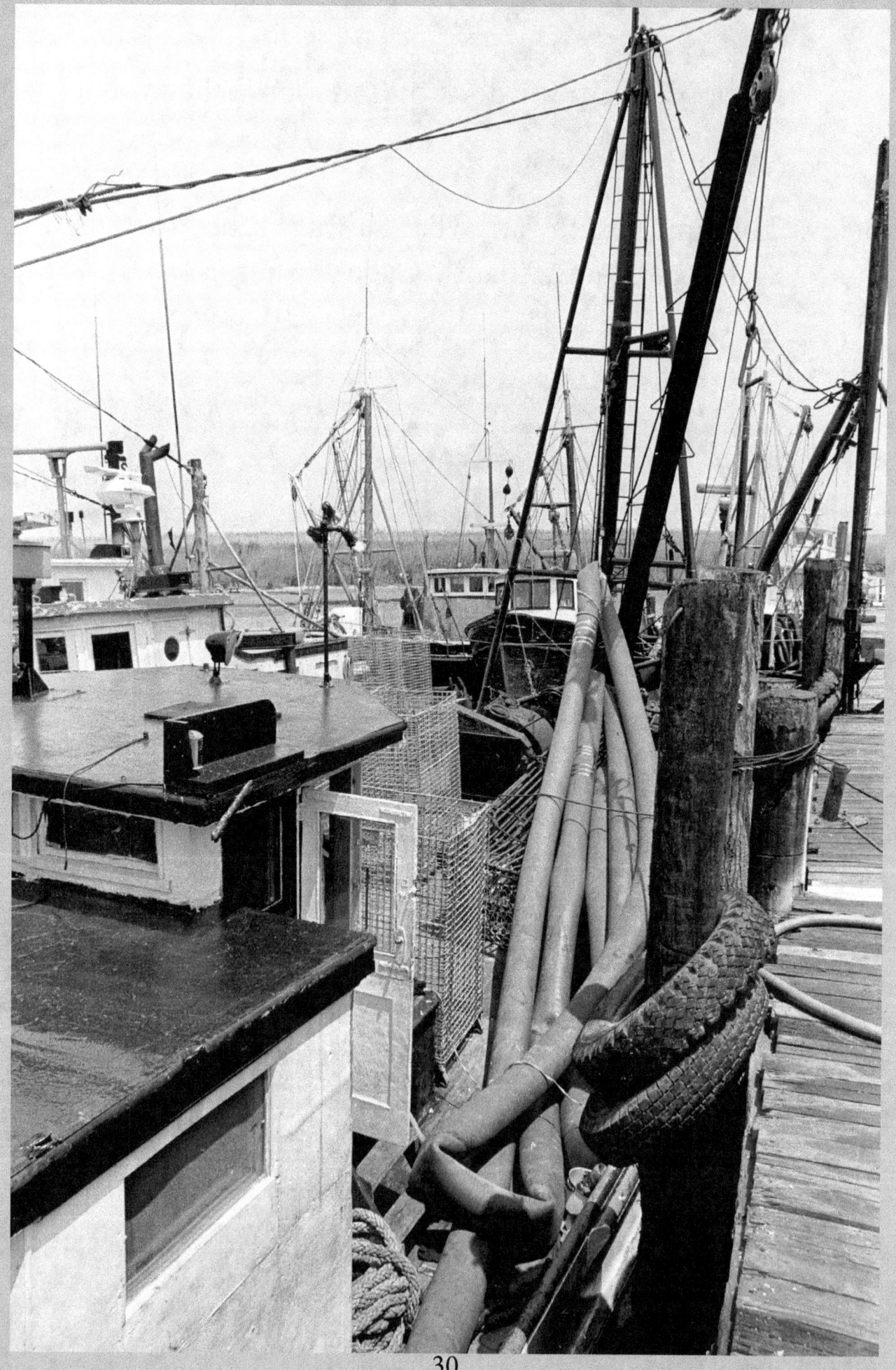

Opposite, below and next two pages: Boats docked along
Will's Hole Thorofare by the "clam factory".

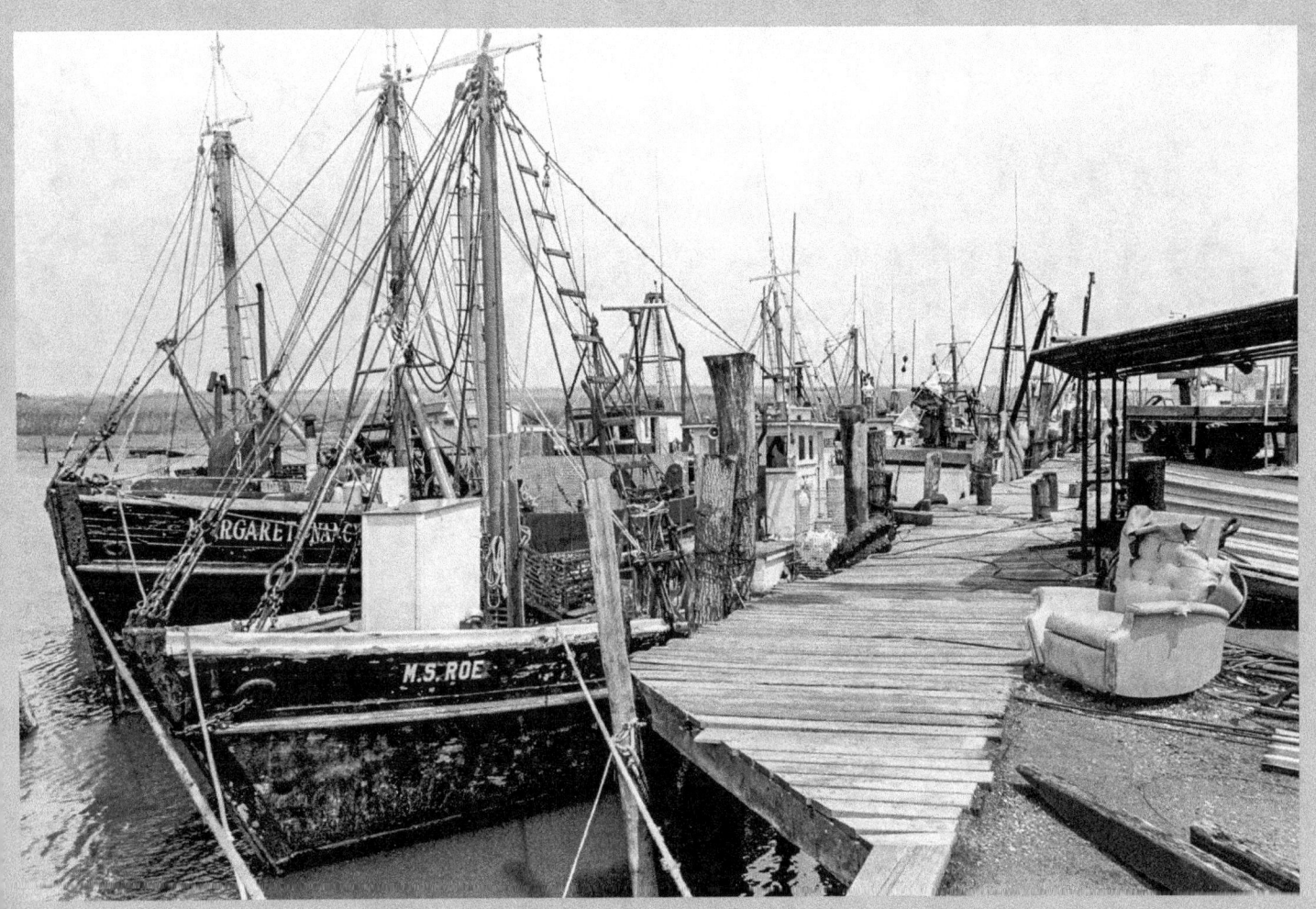

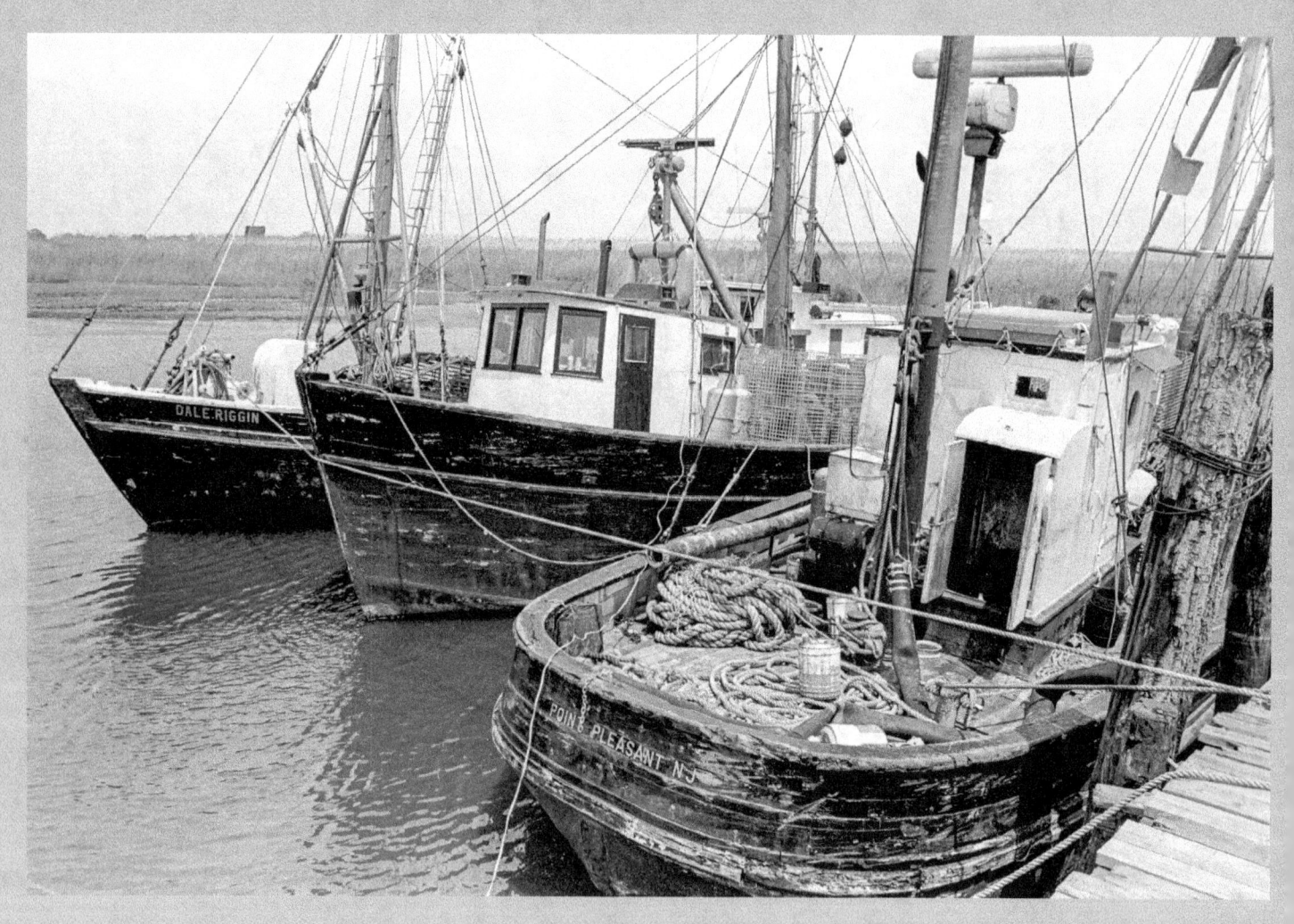

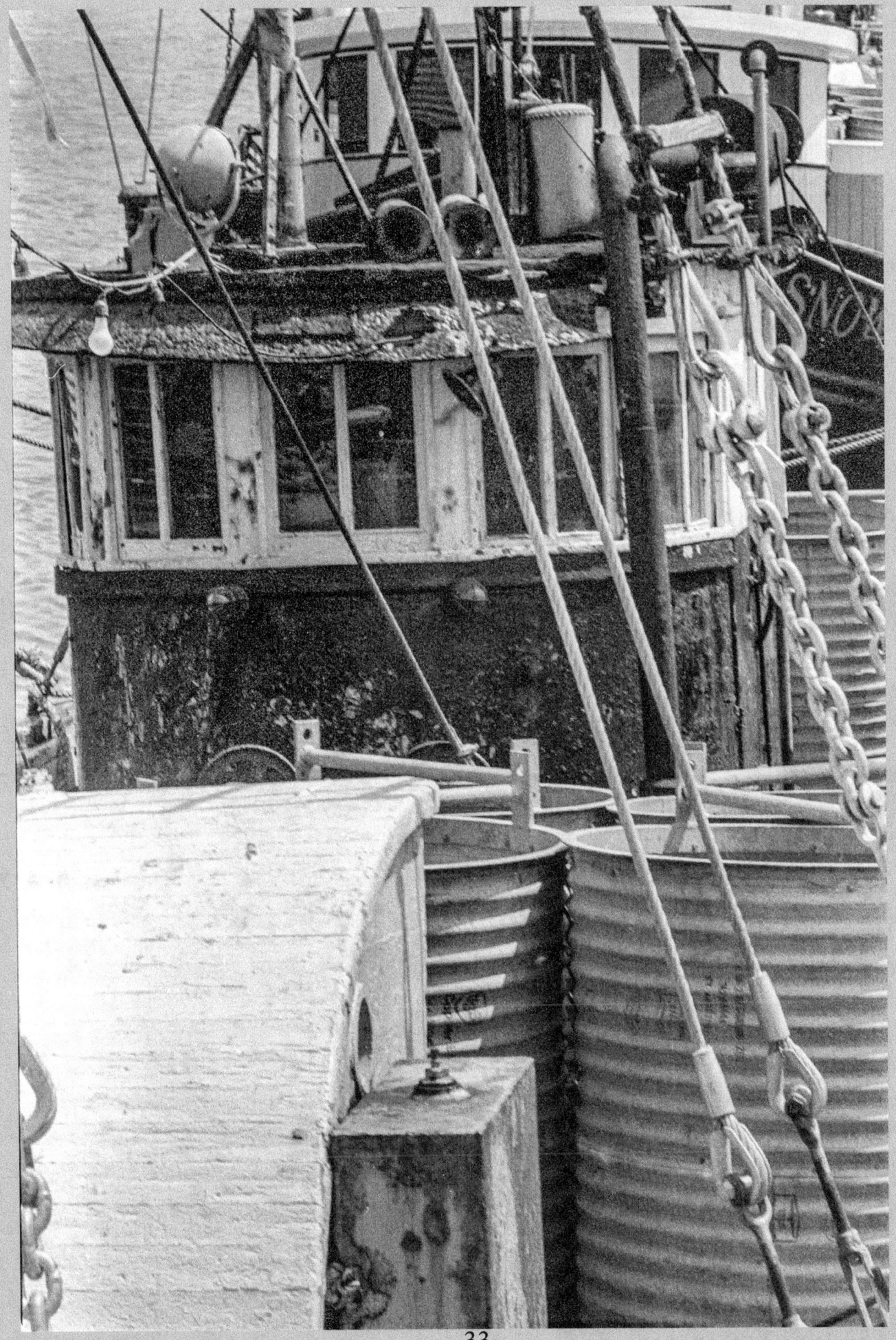

On the west side of the "clam factory" was a large old waterside building surrounded by lobster pots. The following pages show the pots being maintained and loaded onto a lobster boat.

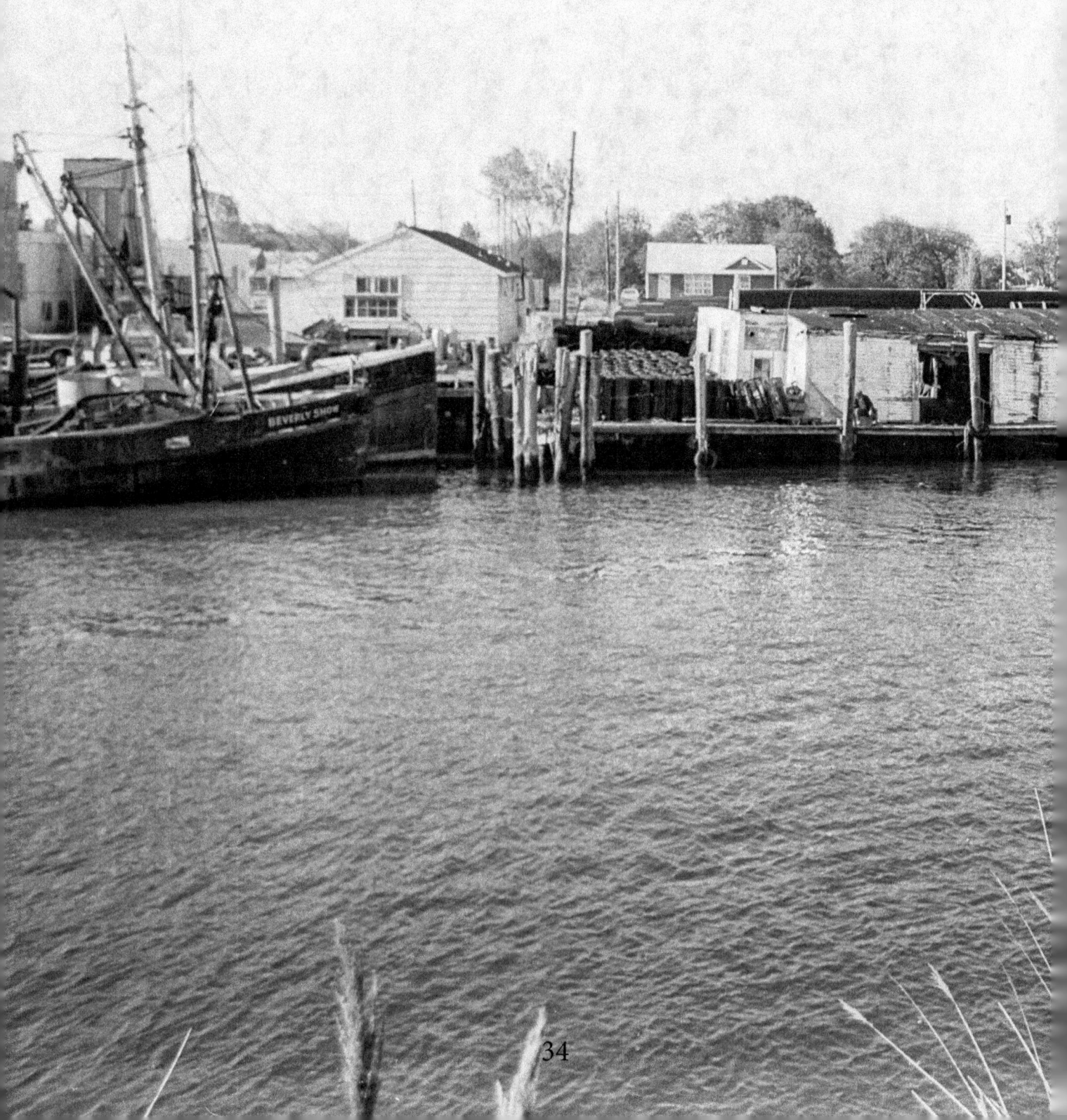

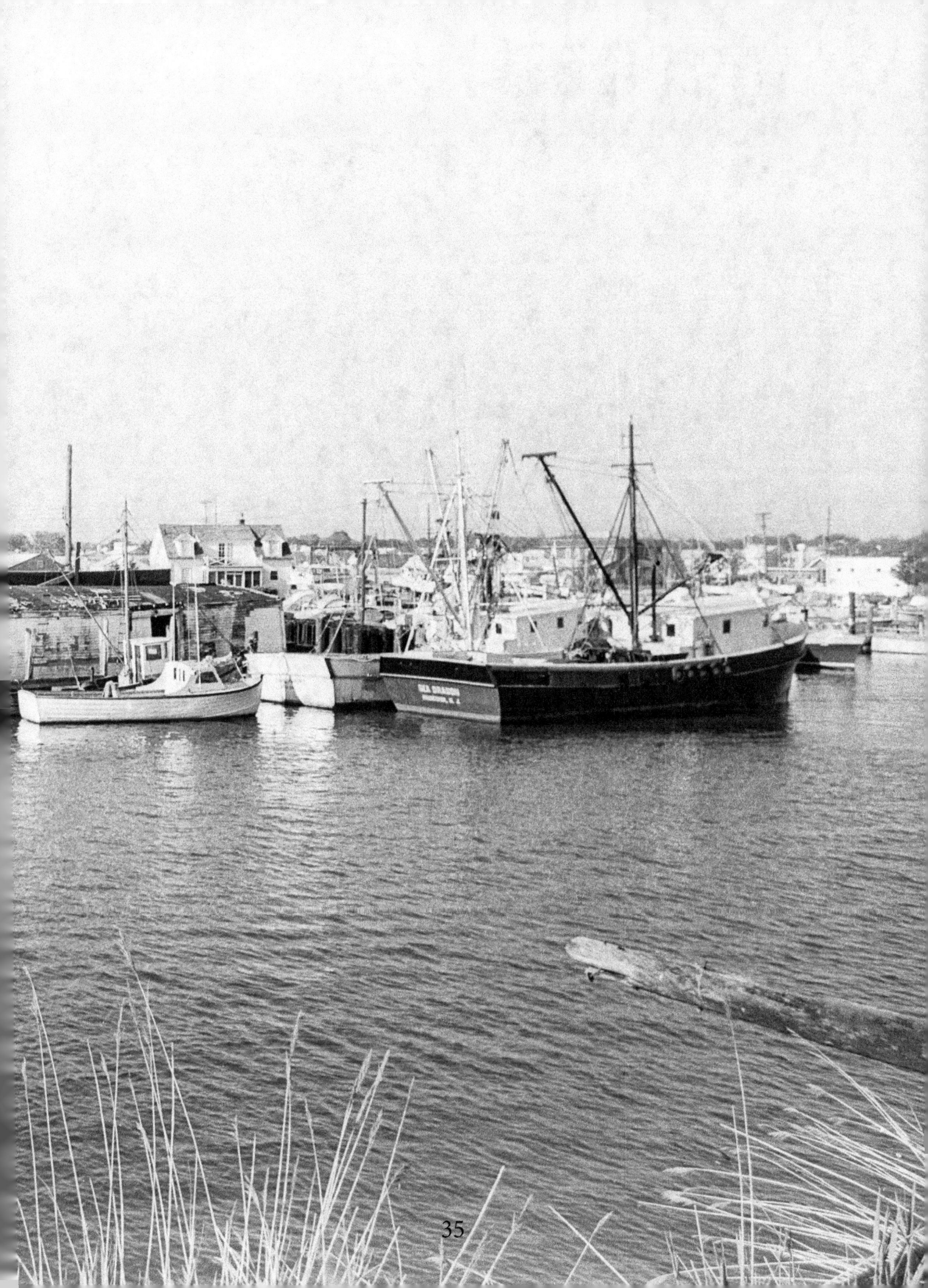

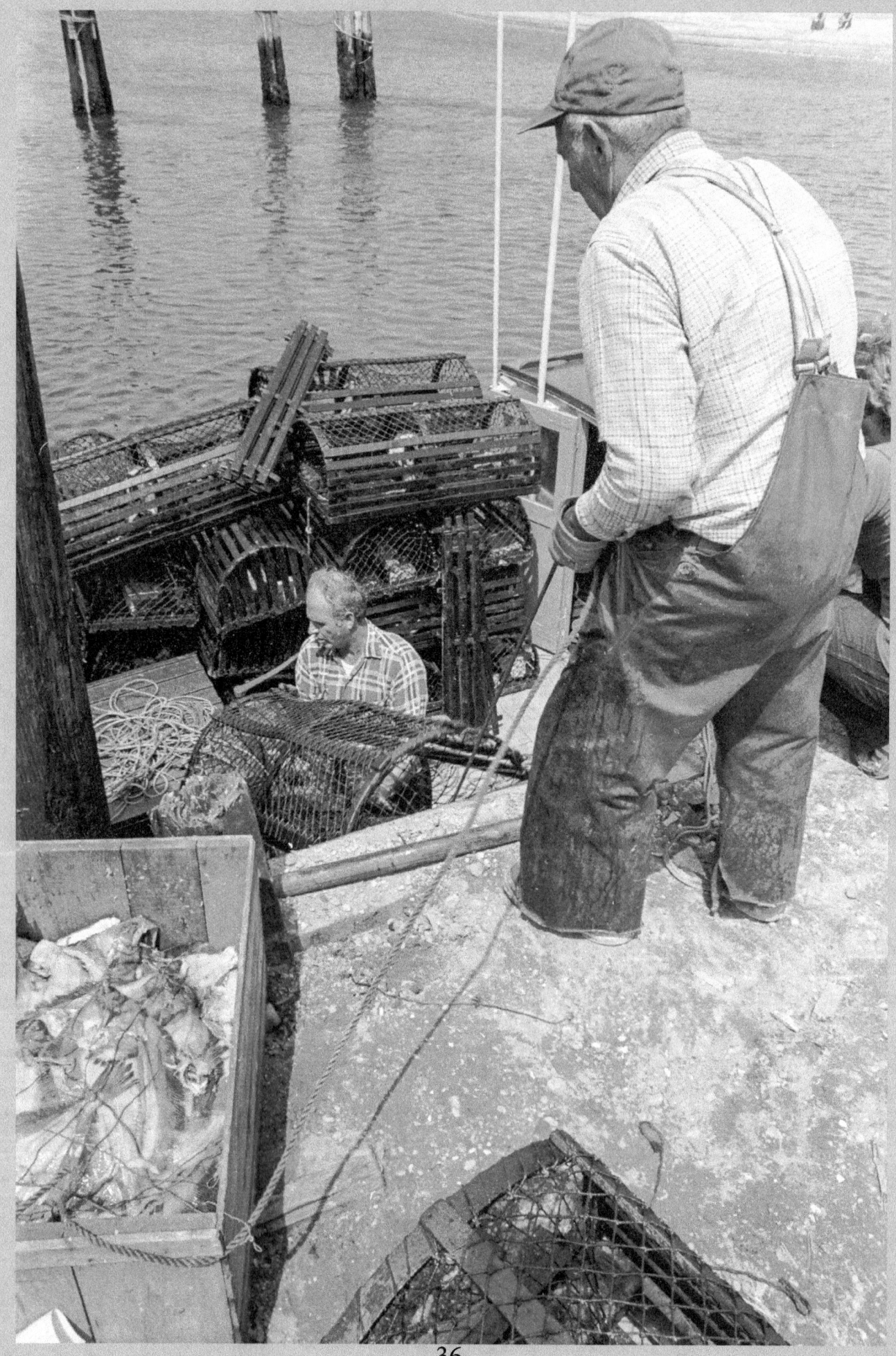

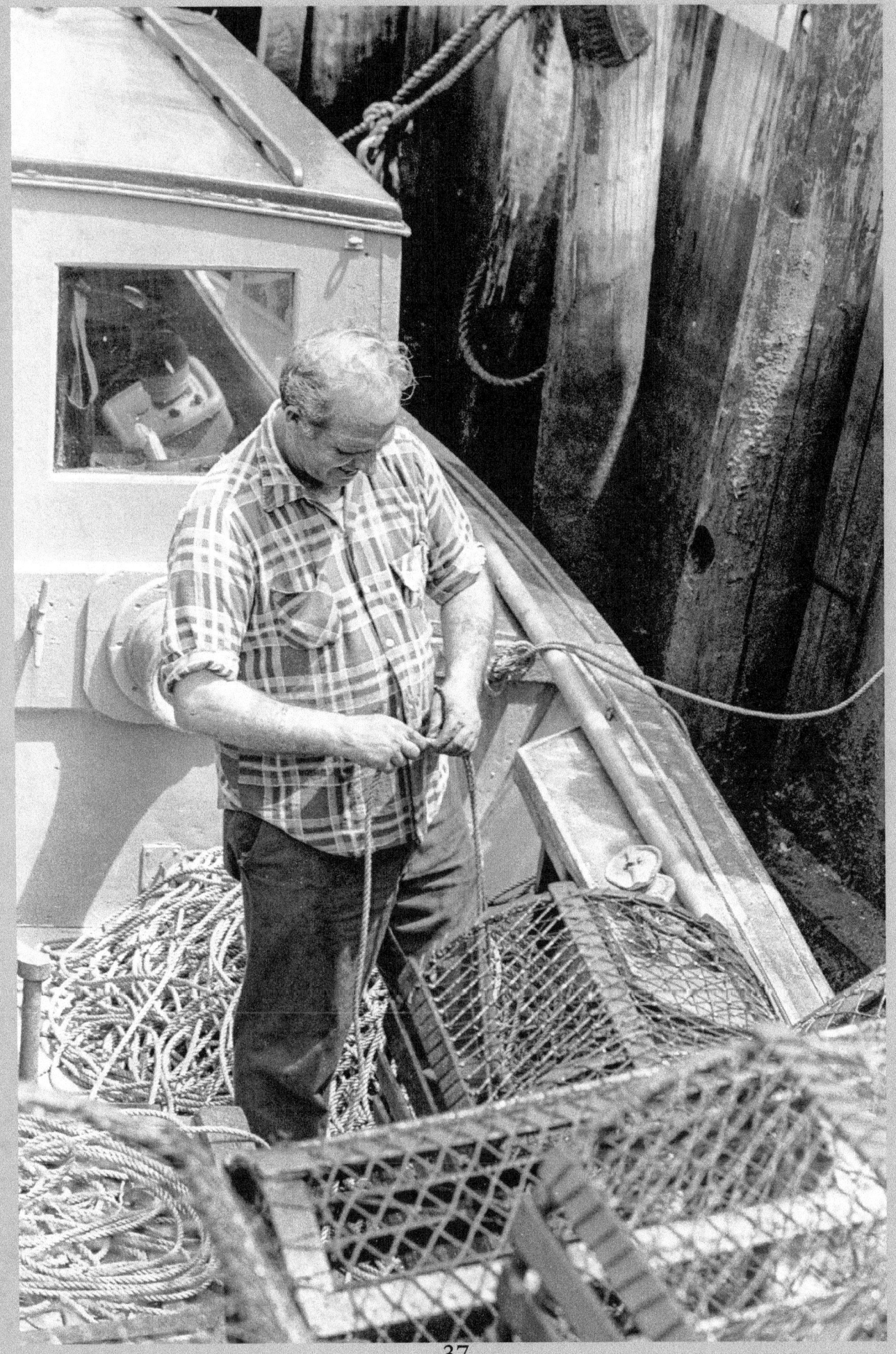

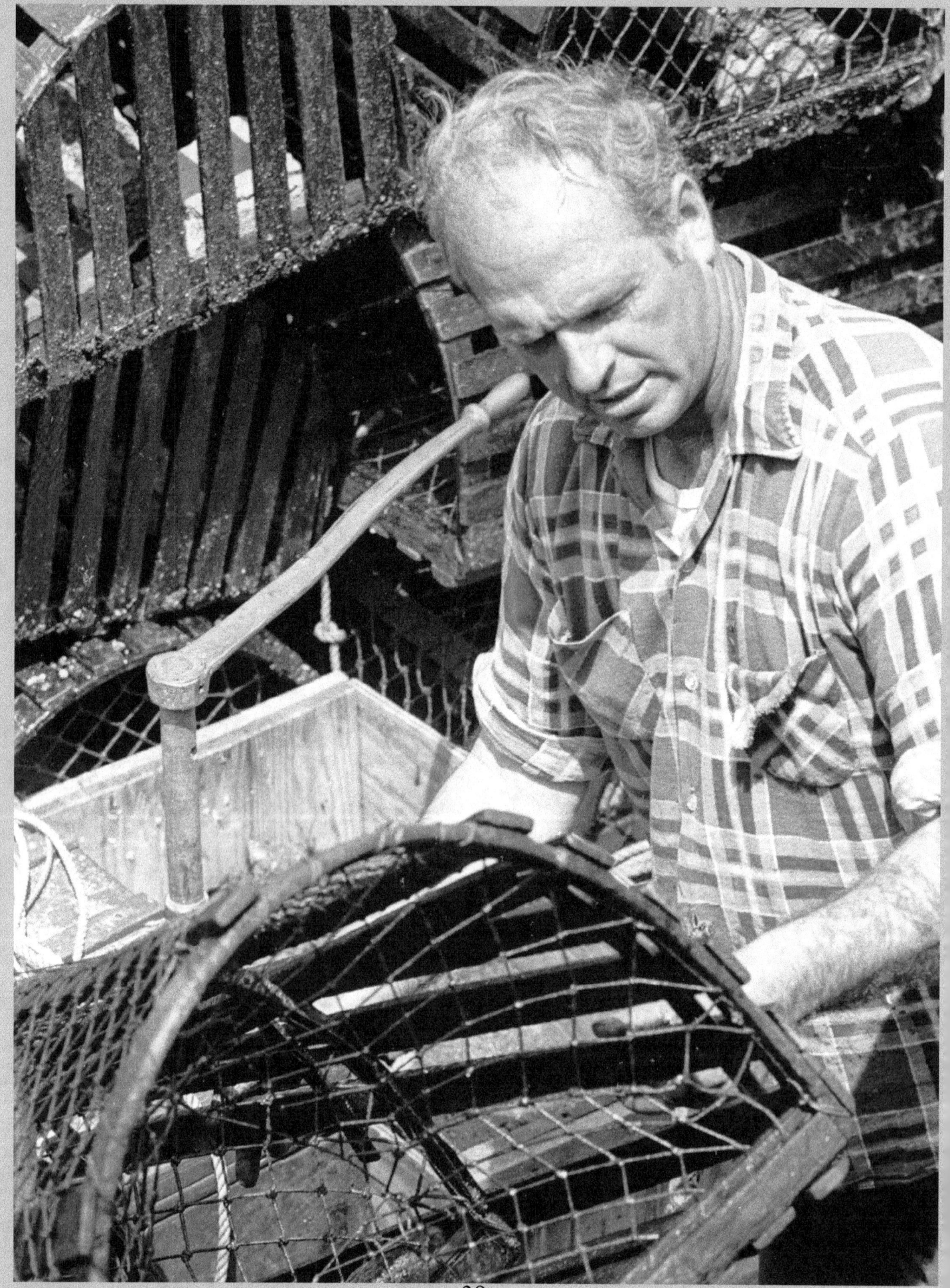

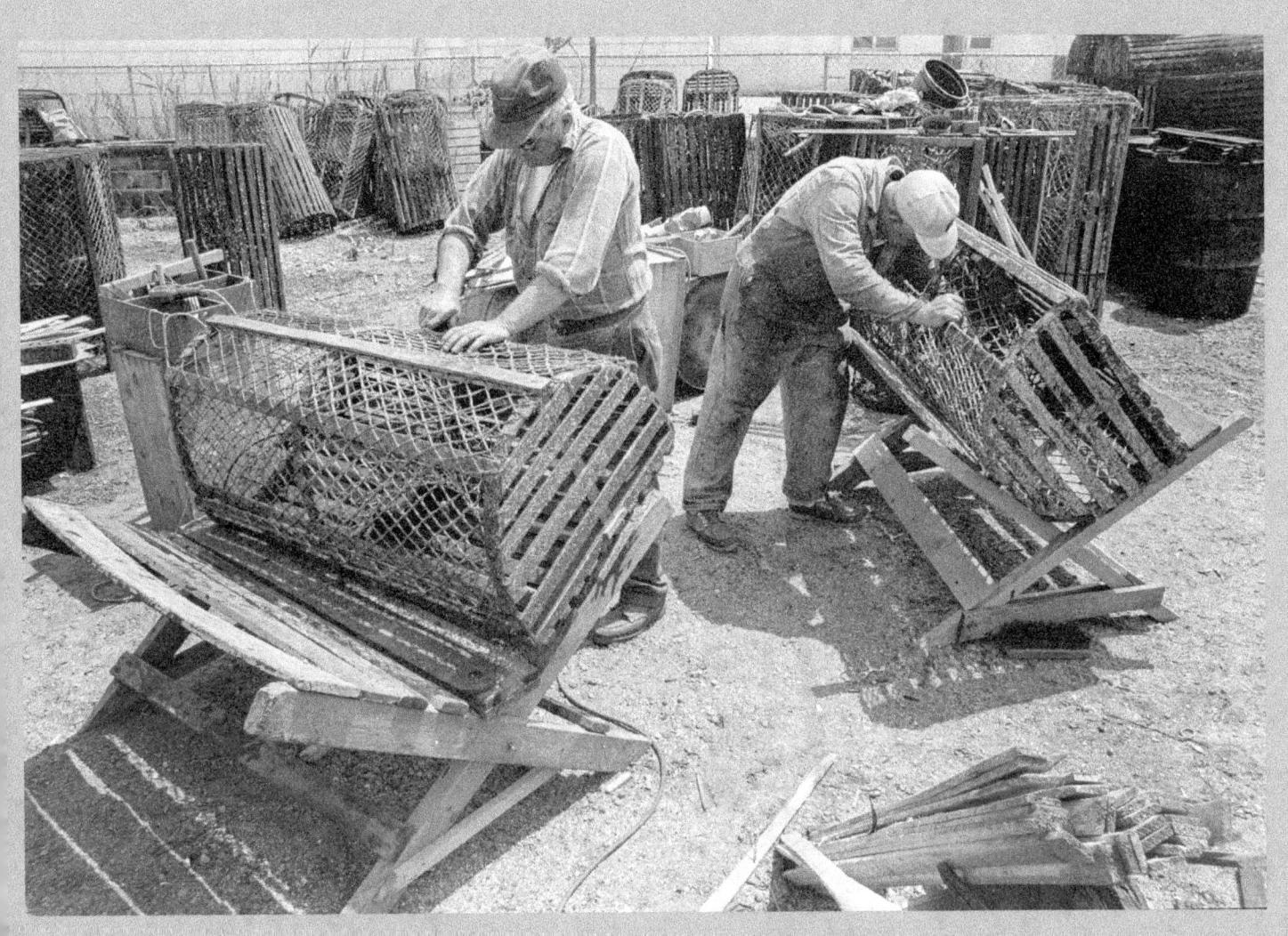

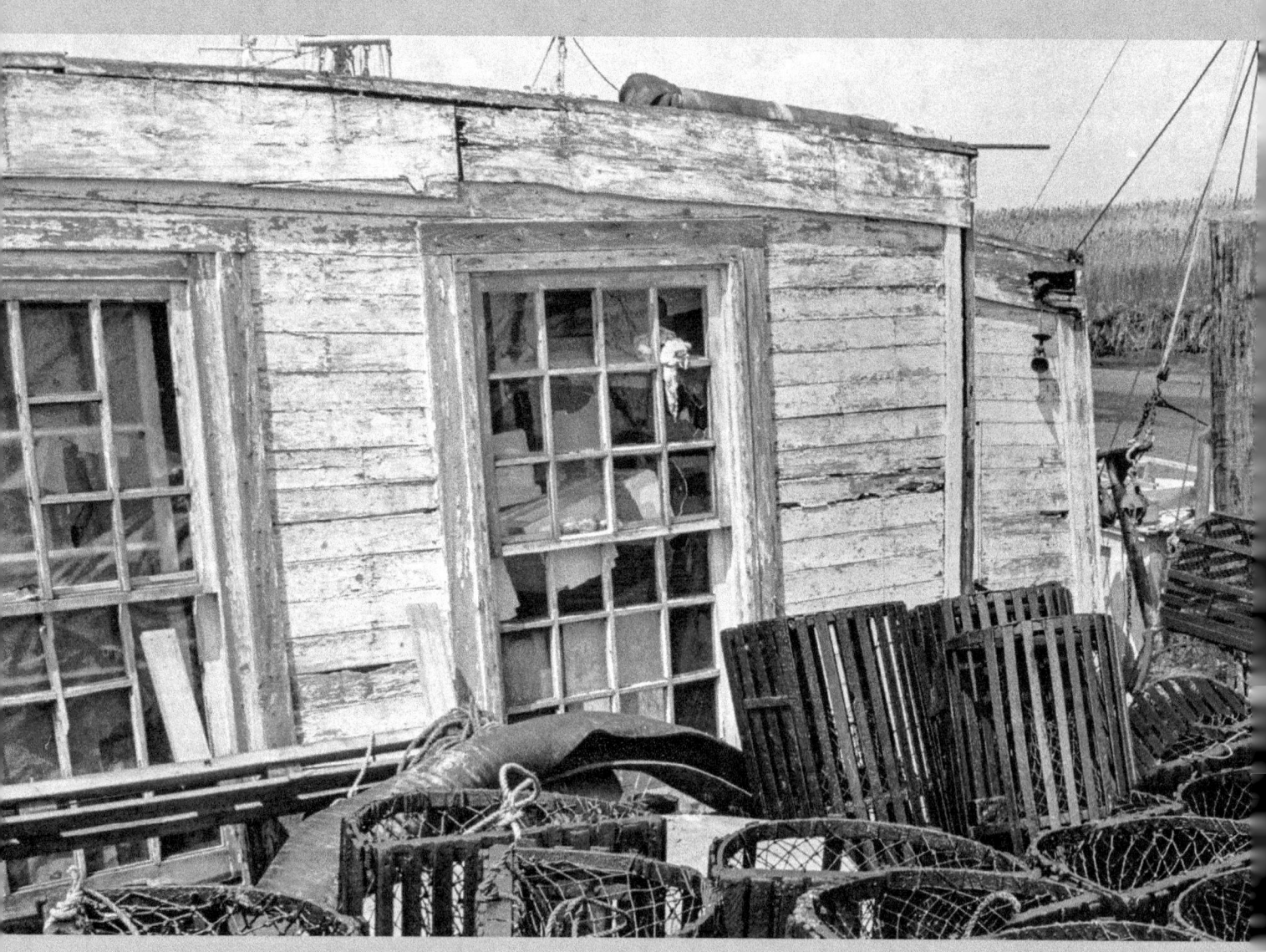

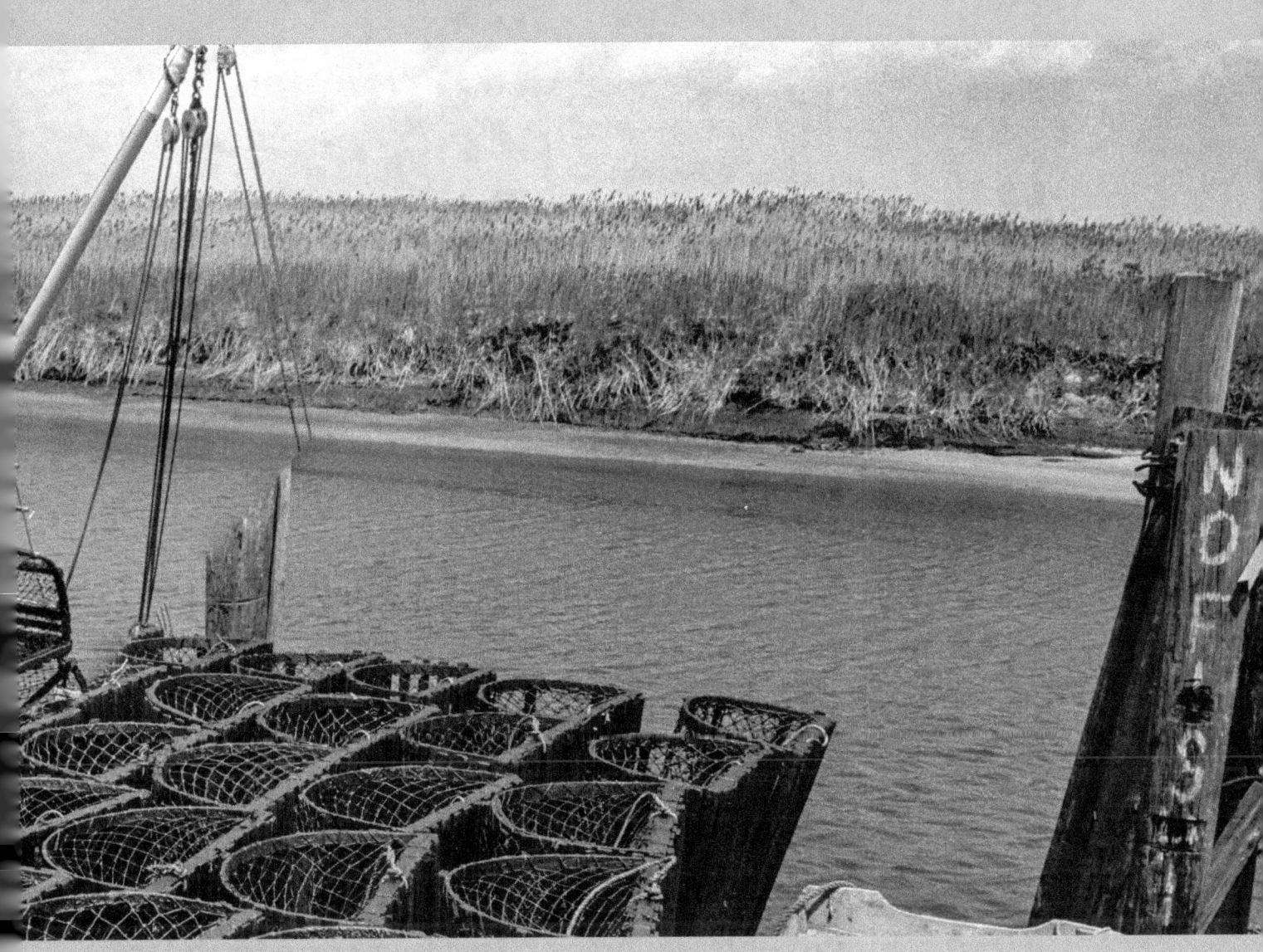

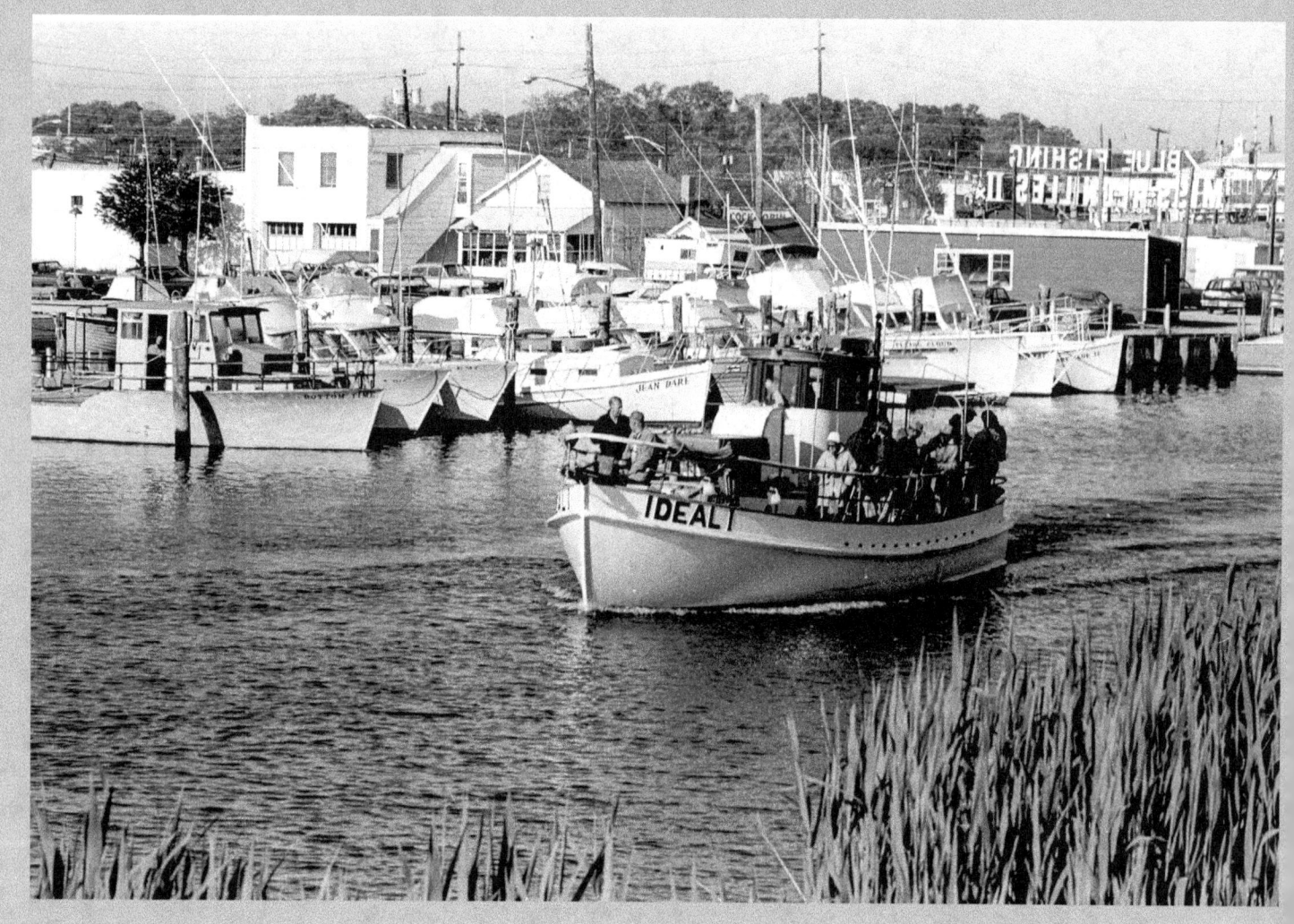

Above: The *Ideal I* going down Will's Hole Thoroughfare with a load of fishermen.

Opposite: Fishing boats docked at Will's Hole with a Central Railroad of New Jersey passenger train in the background.

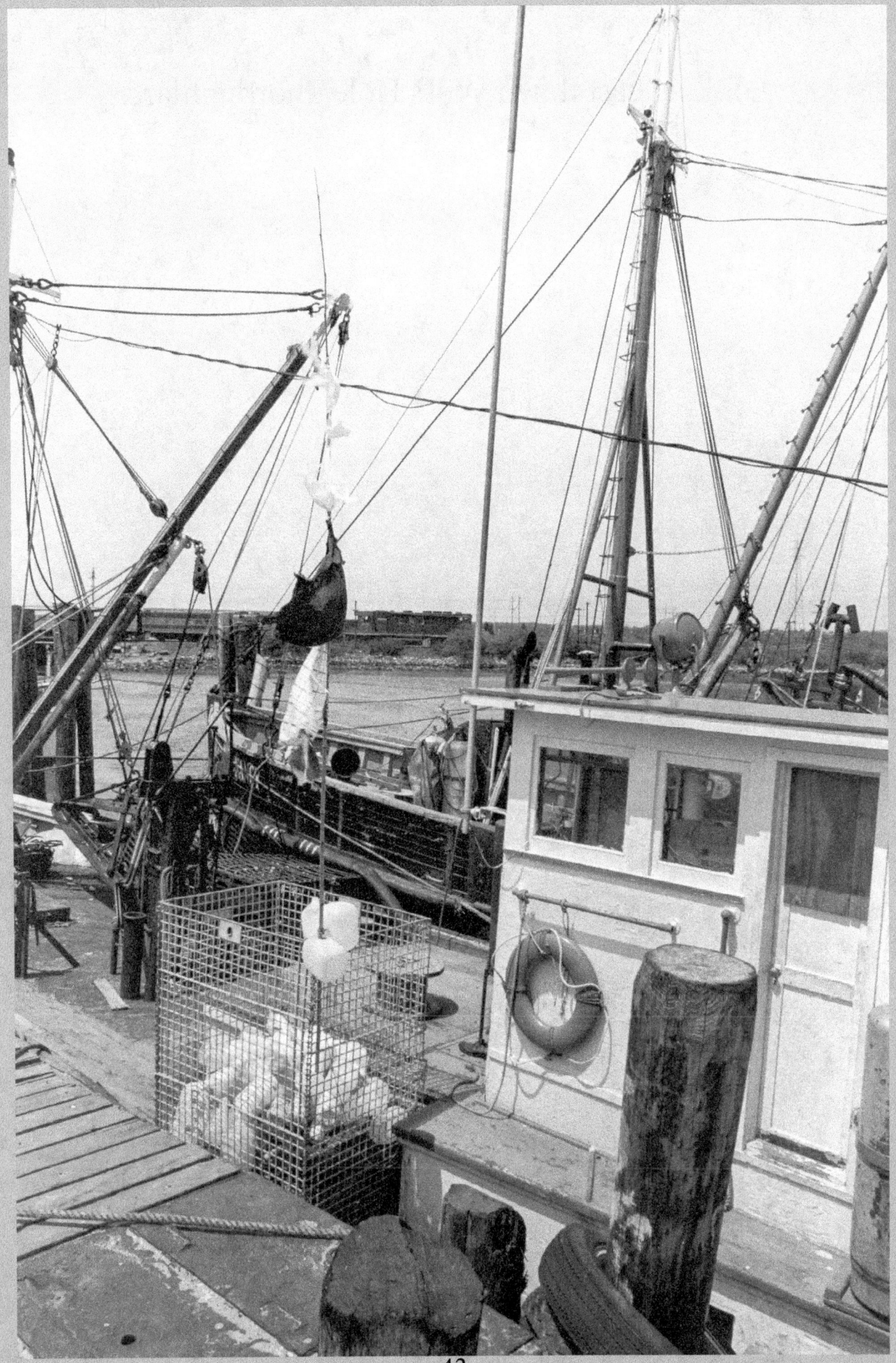

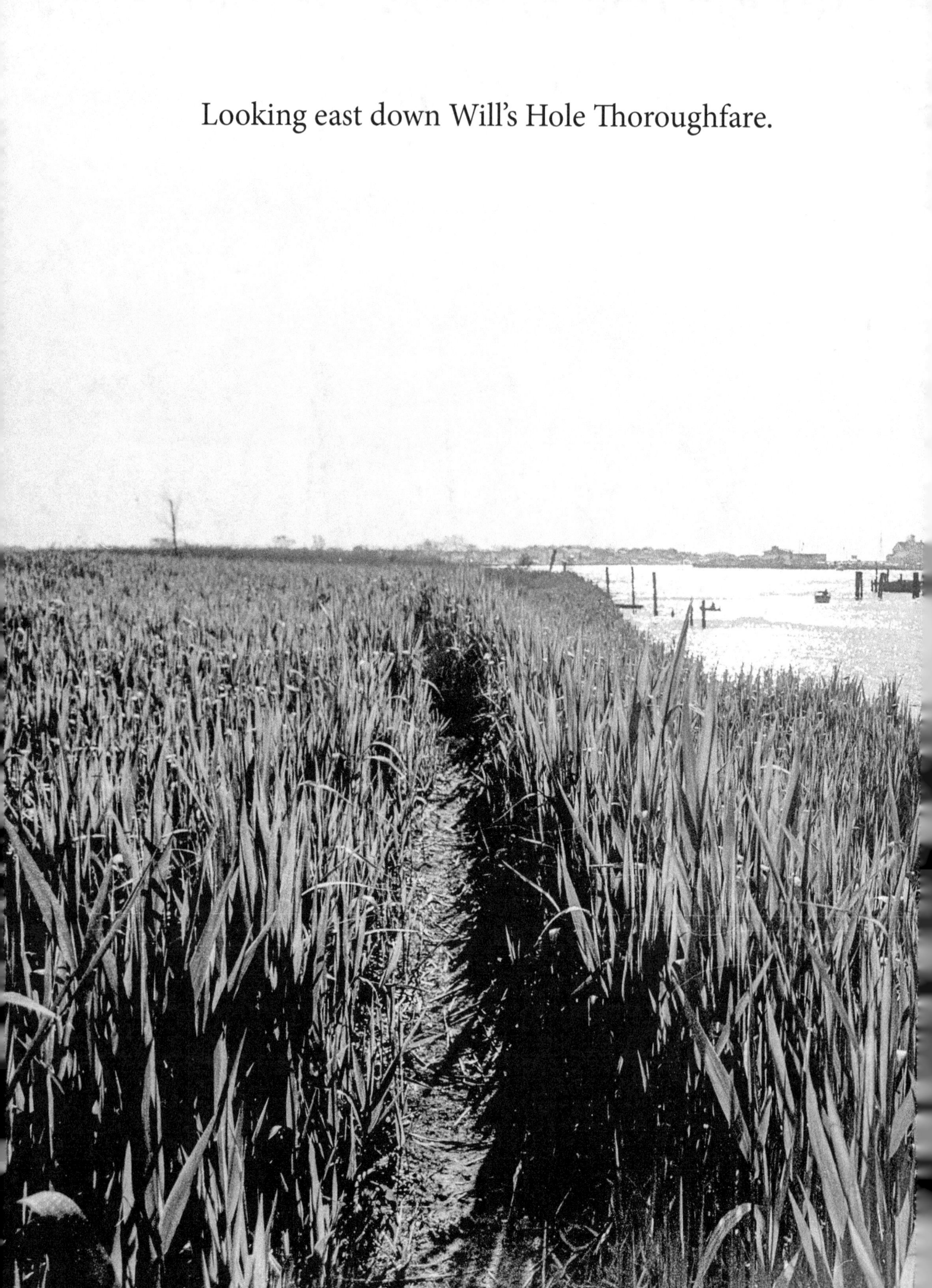

Looking east down Will's Hole Thoroughfare.

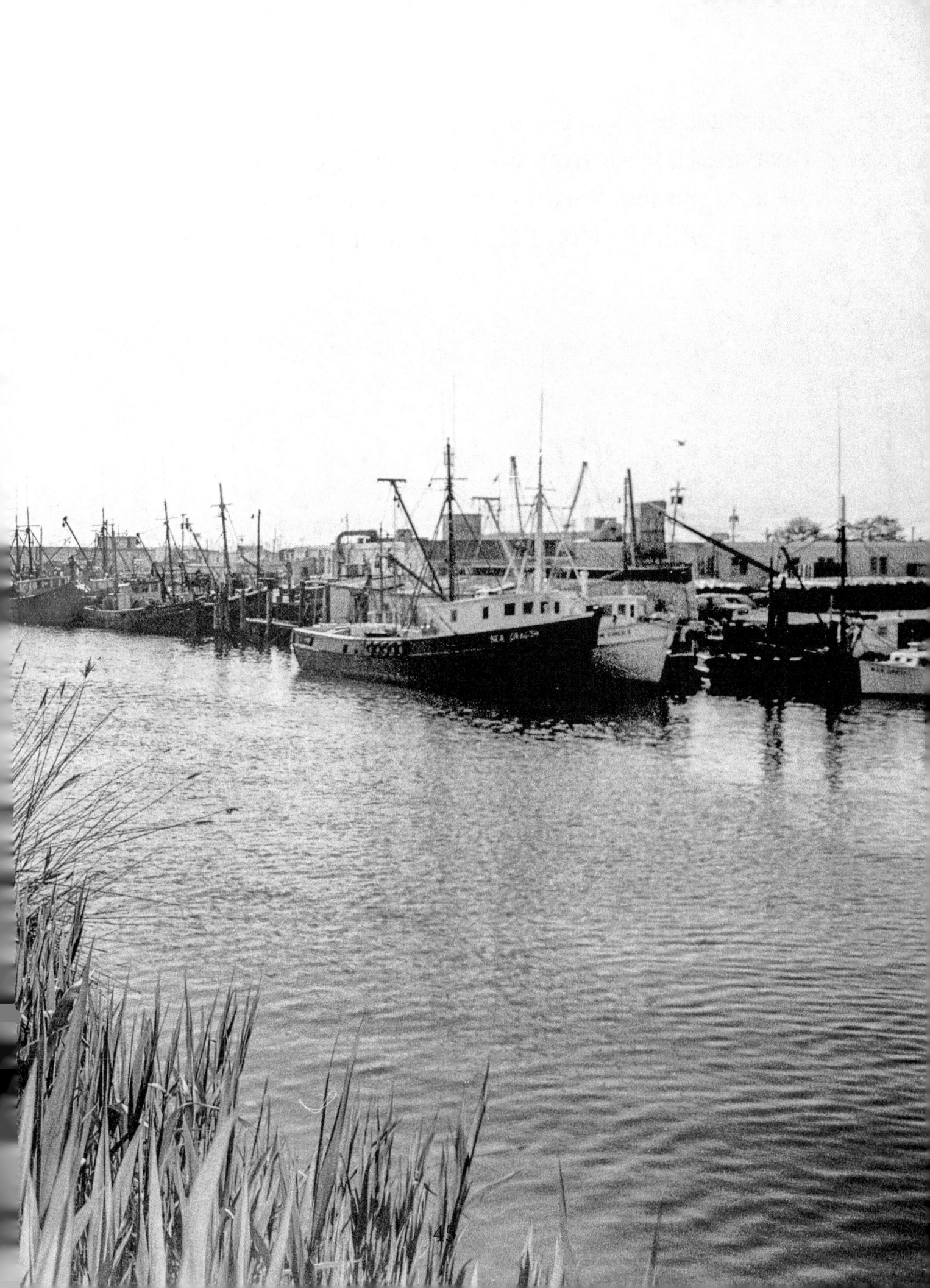

I took a series of photographs one cold winter morning just after a fresh snowstorm. Looking down Cooks Creek, the expanded Shrimp Box is under construction on the right with the Coast Guard Station in the background.

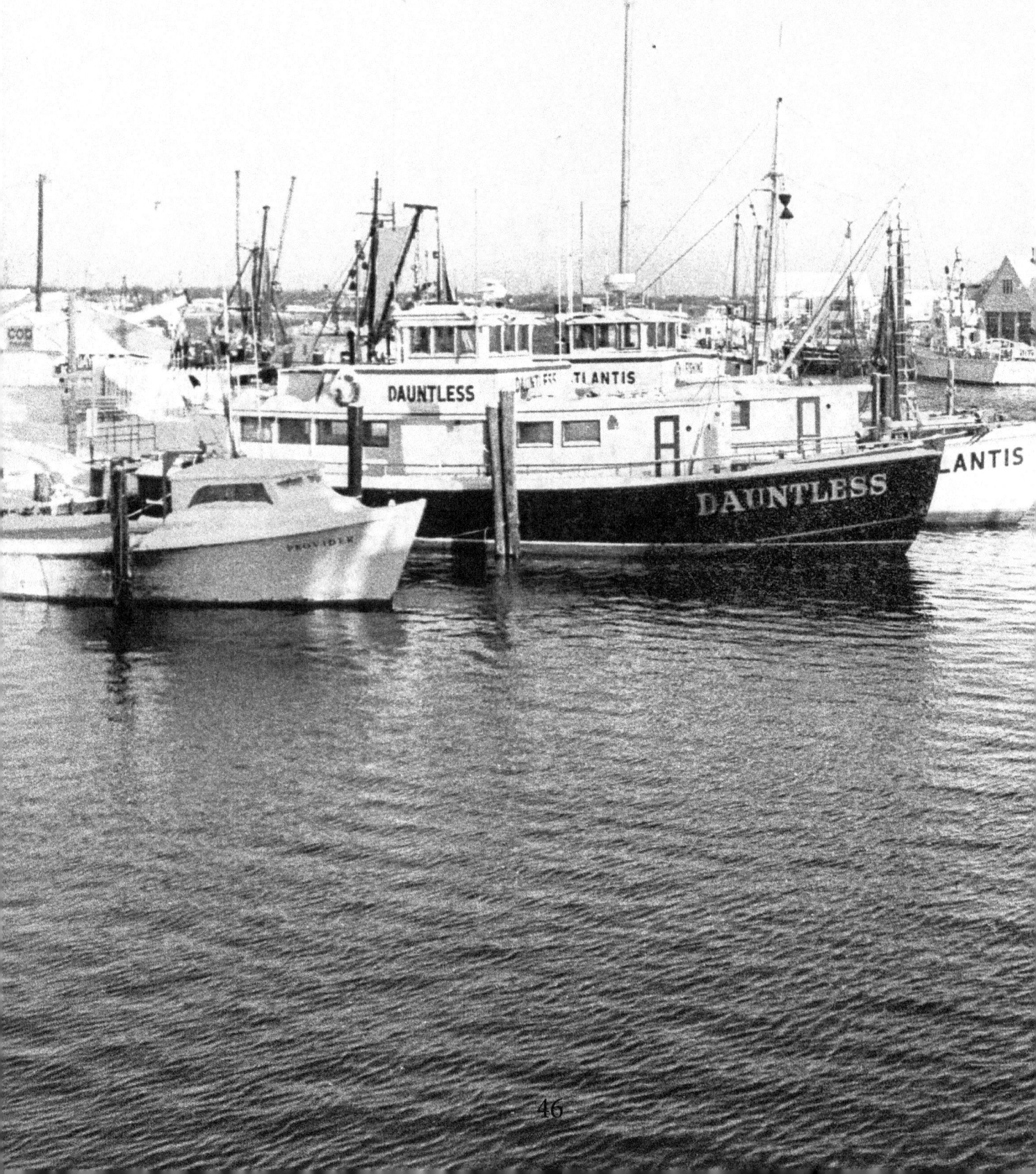

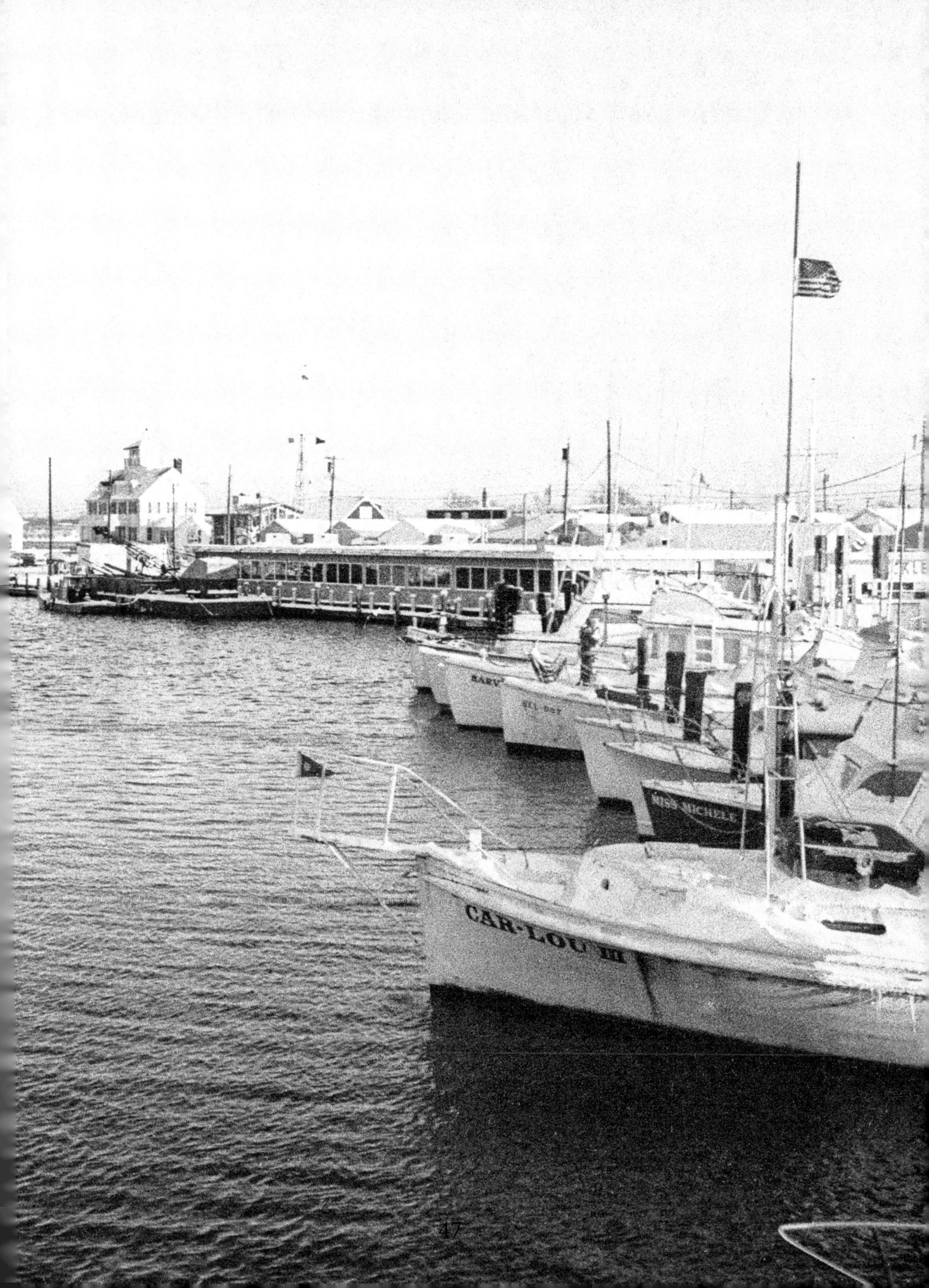

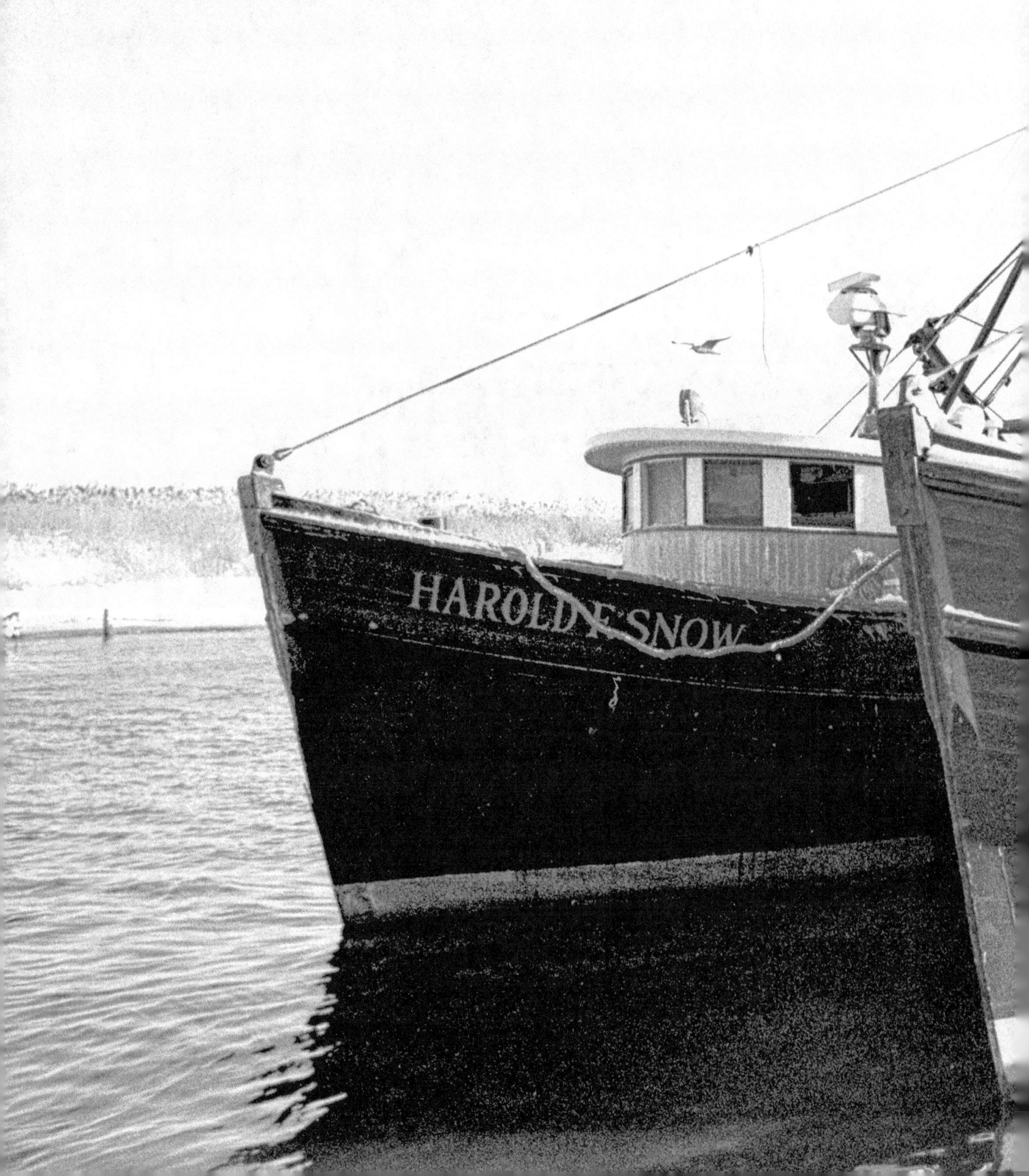

The *Harold F. Snow* and *Cora-May Snow* in the snow.

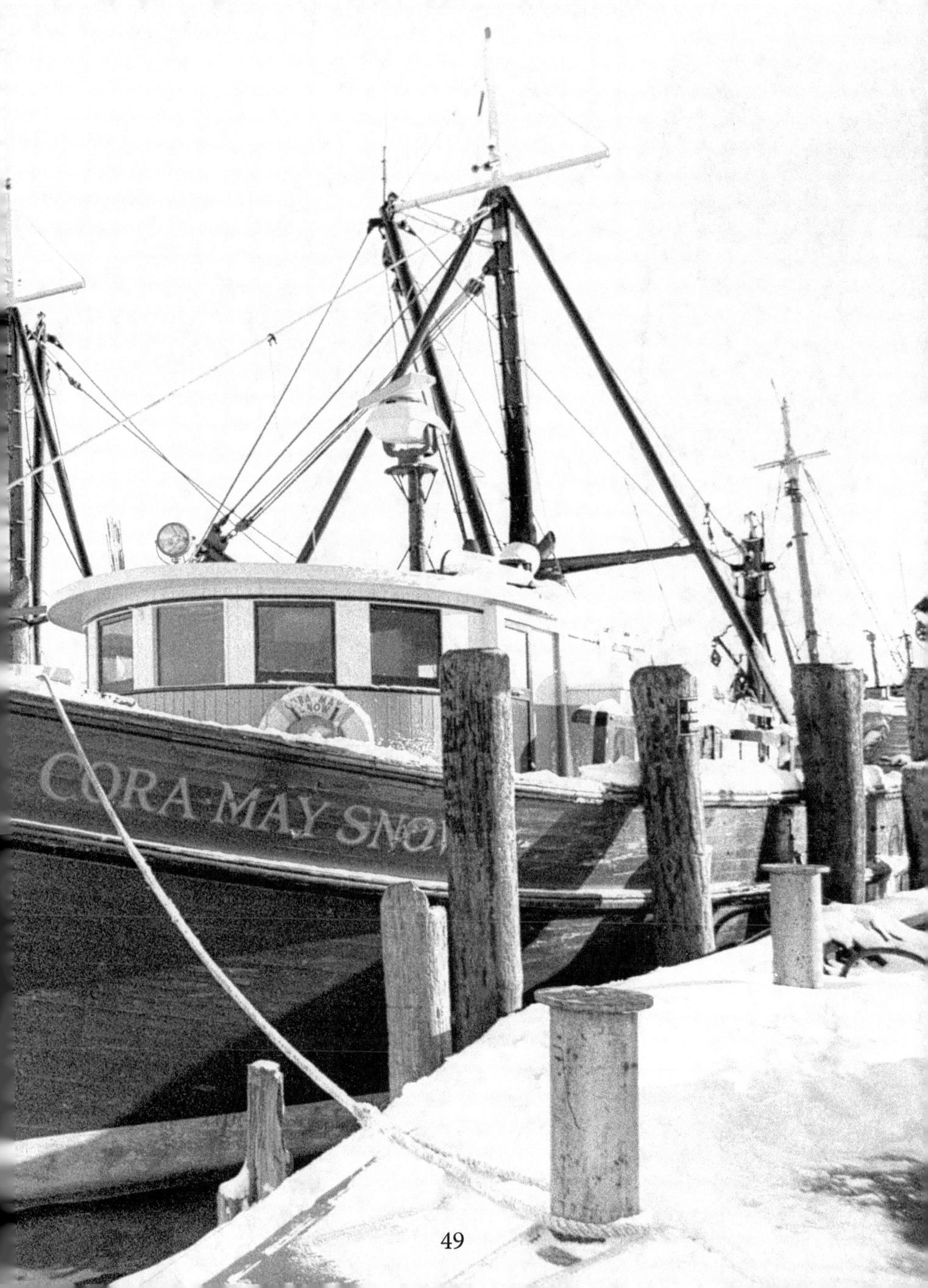

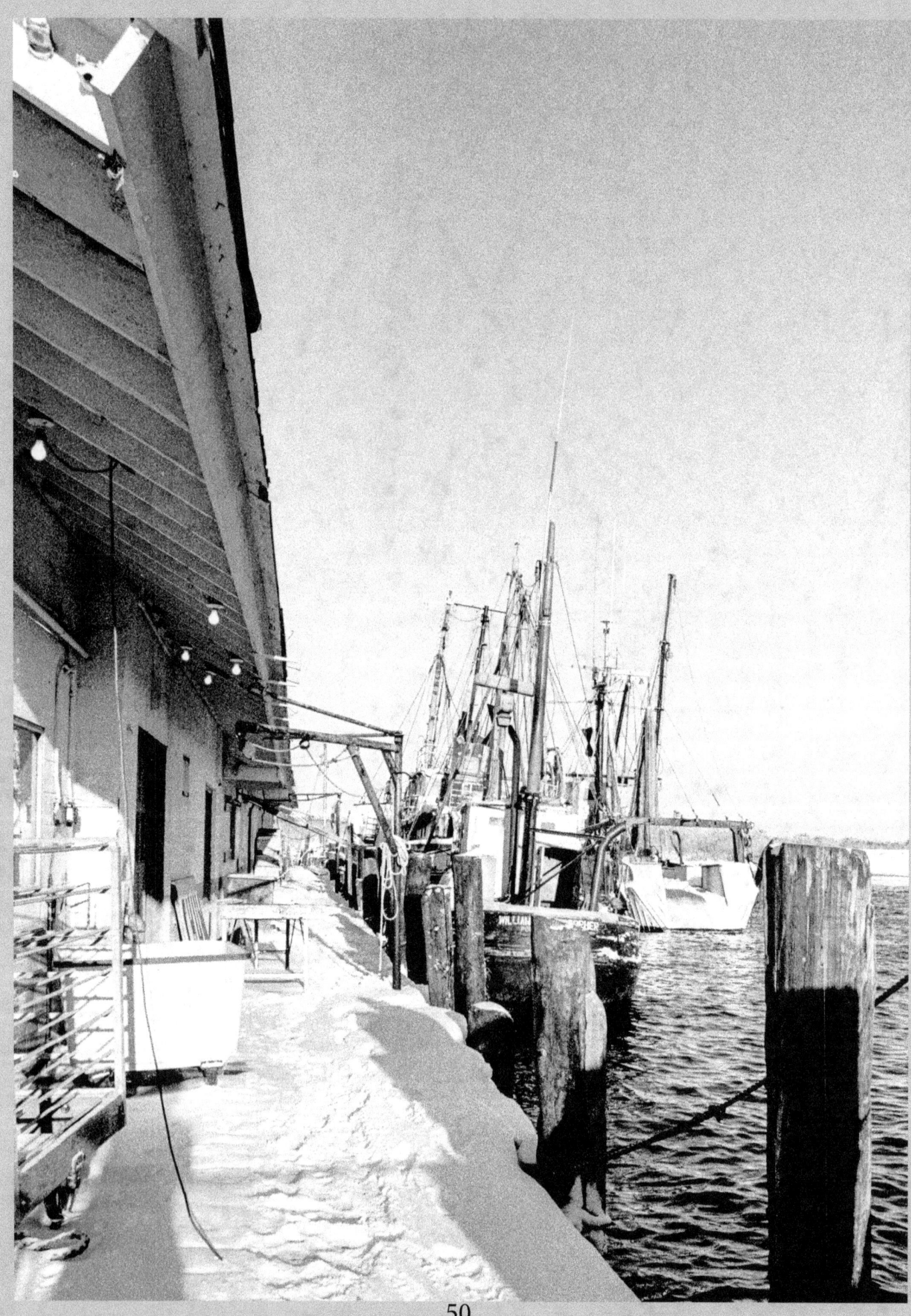

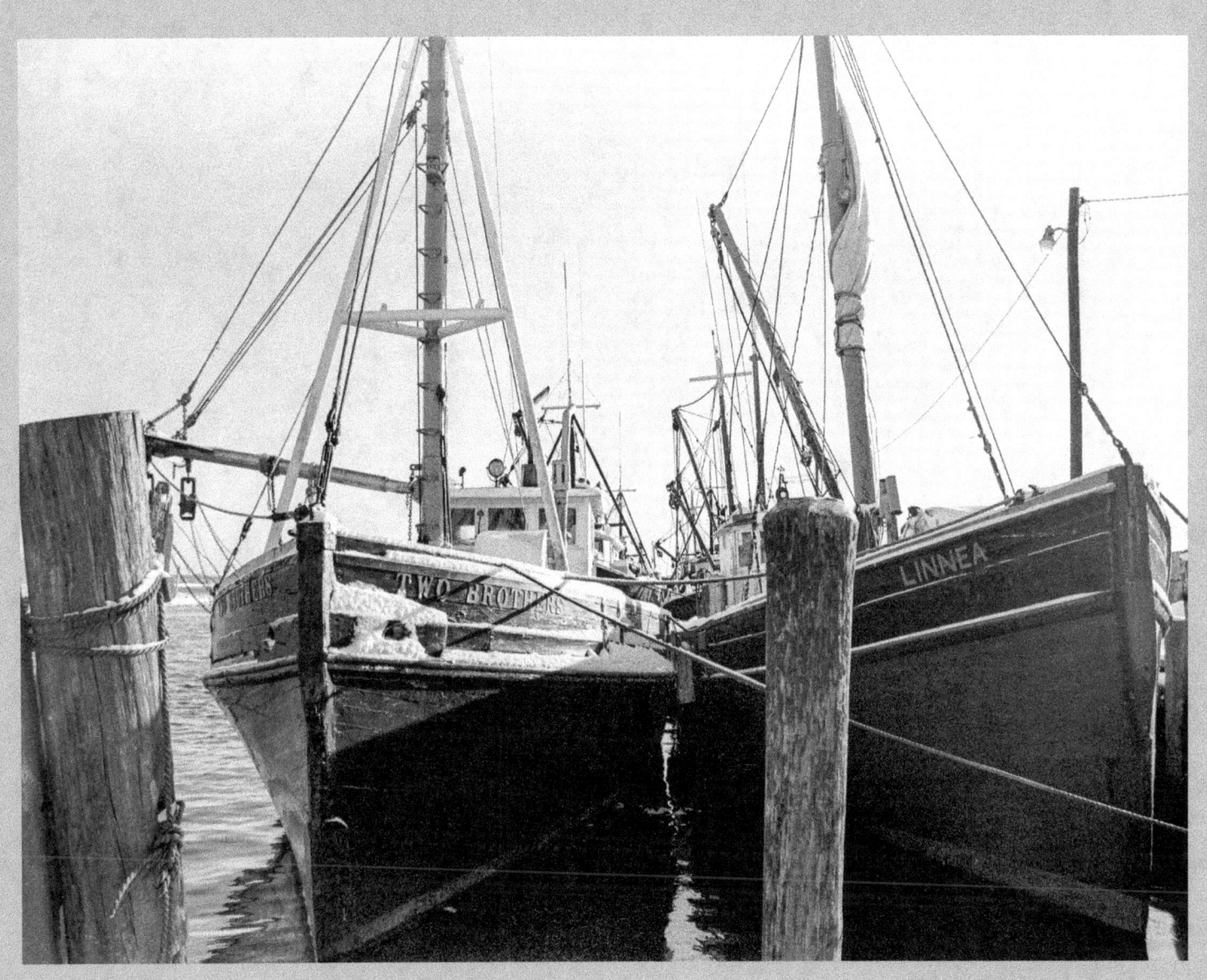

Opposite and Above: Carlson's Fishery in the snow.

Coast Guard Station, Manasquan Inlet, and cutter *Point Batan*. The *Point Batan* was stationed here from 1966 - 1984.

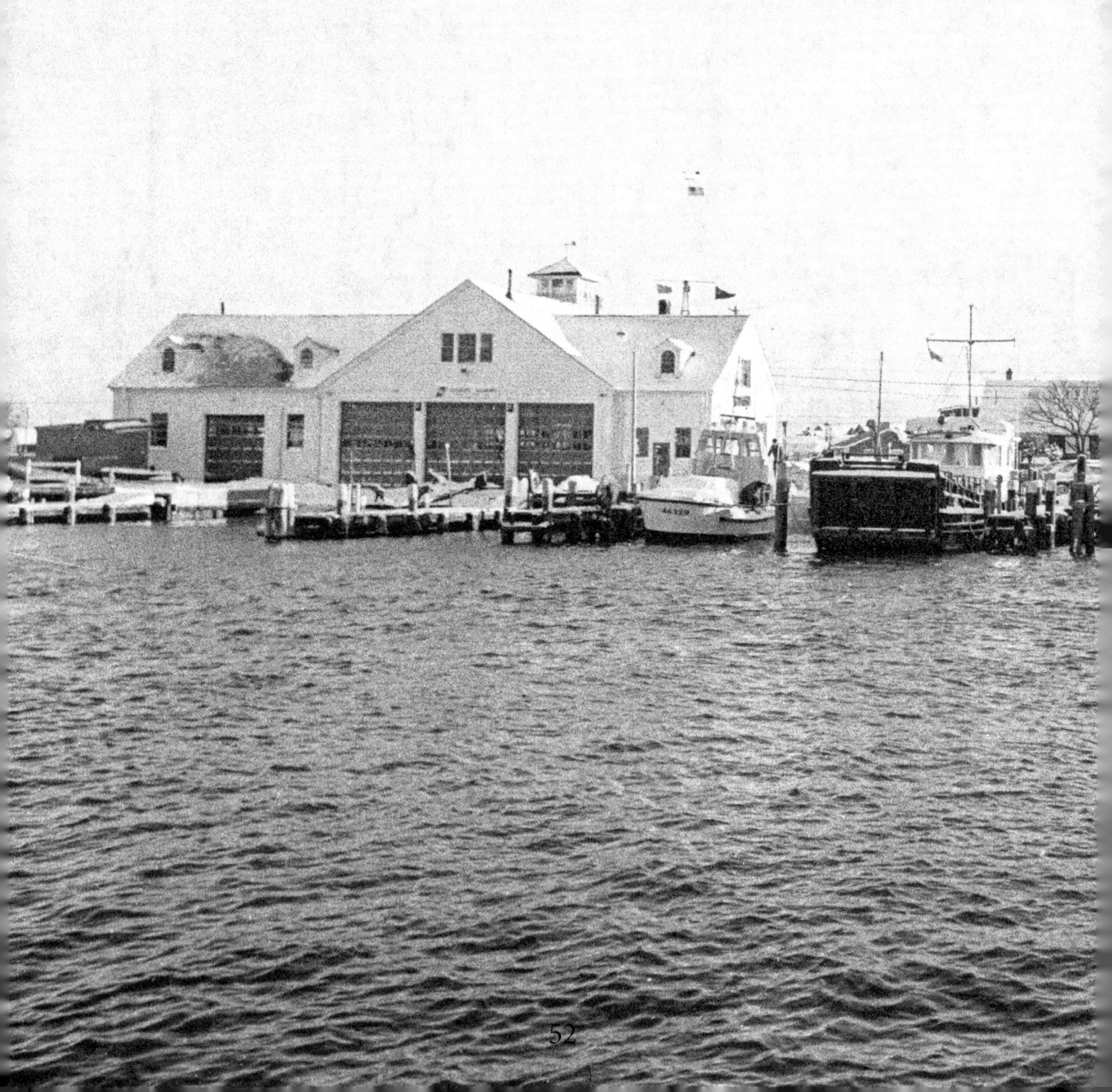

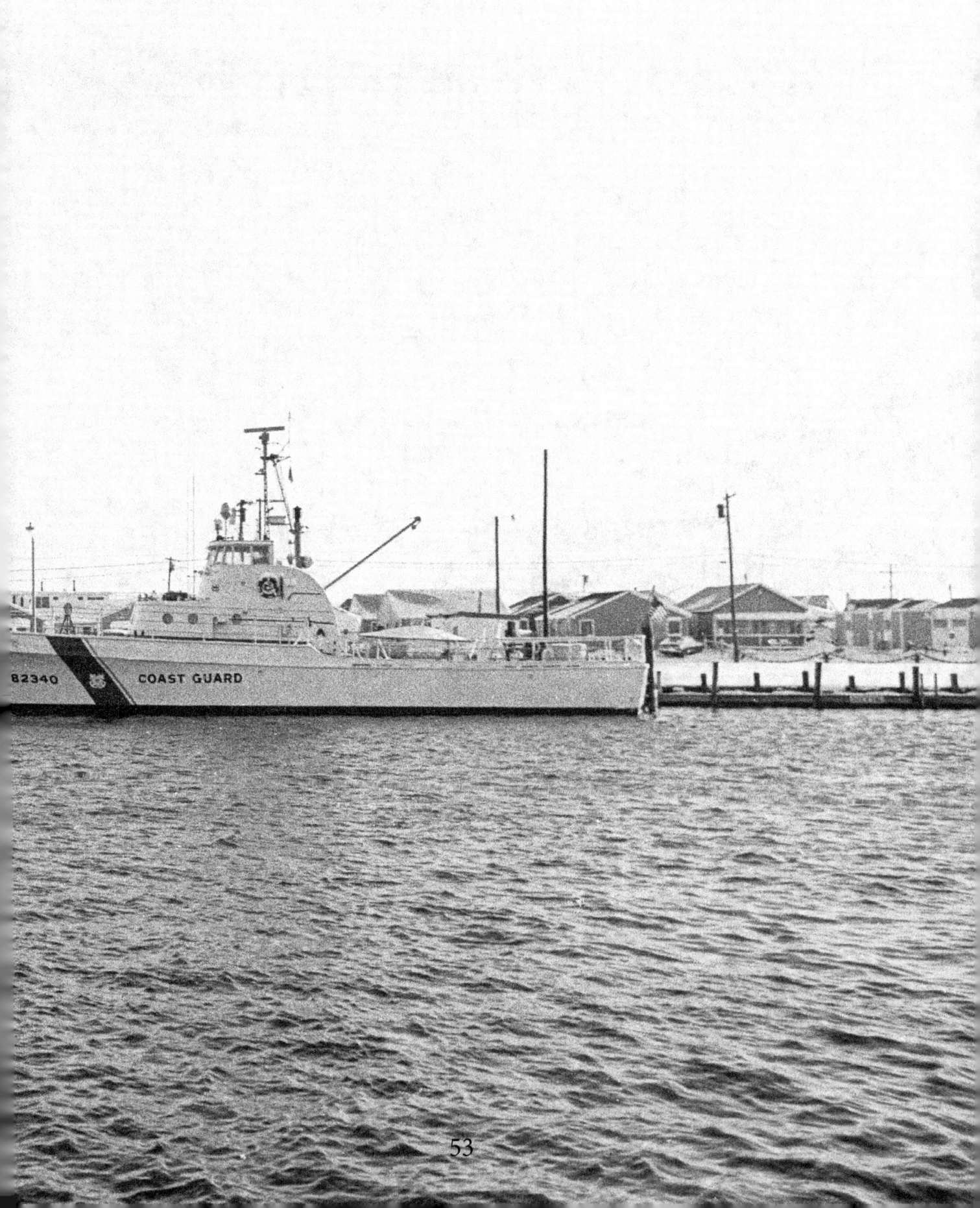

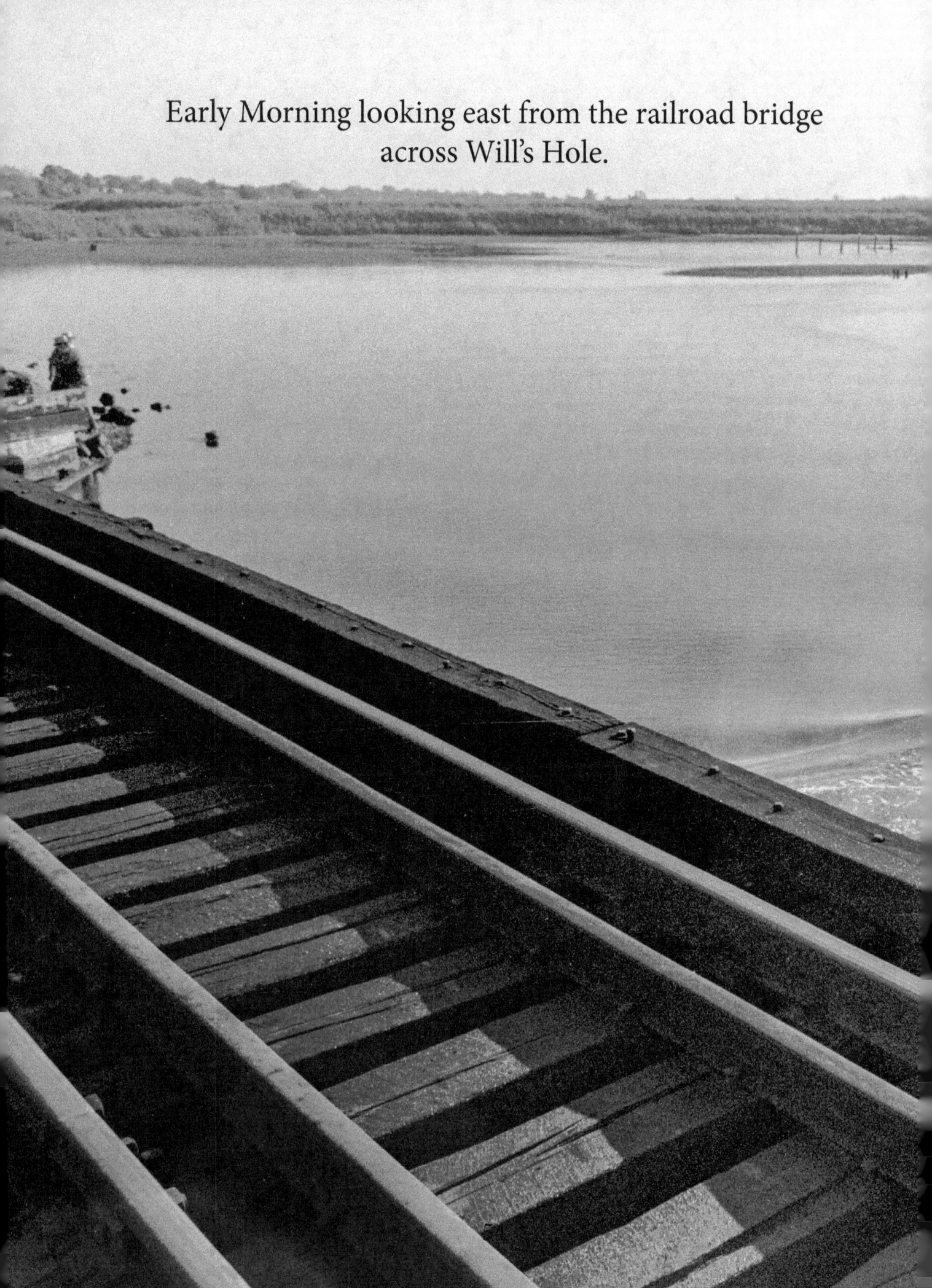

Early Morning looking east from the railroad bridge across Will's Hole.

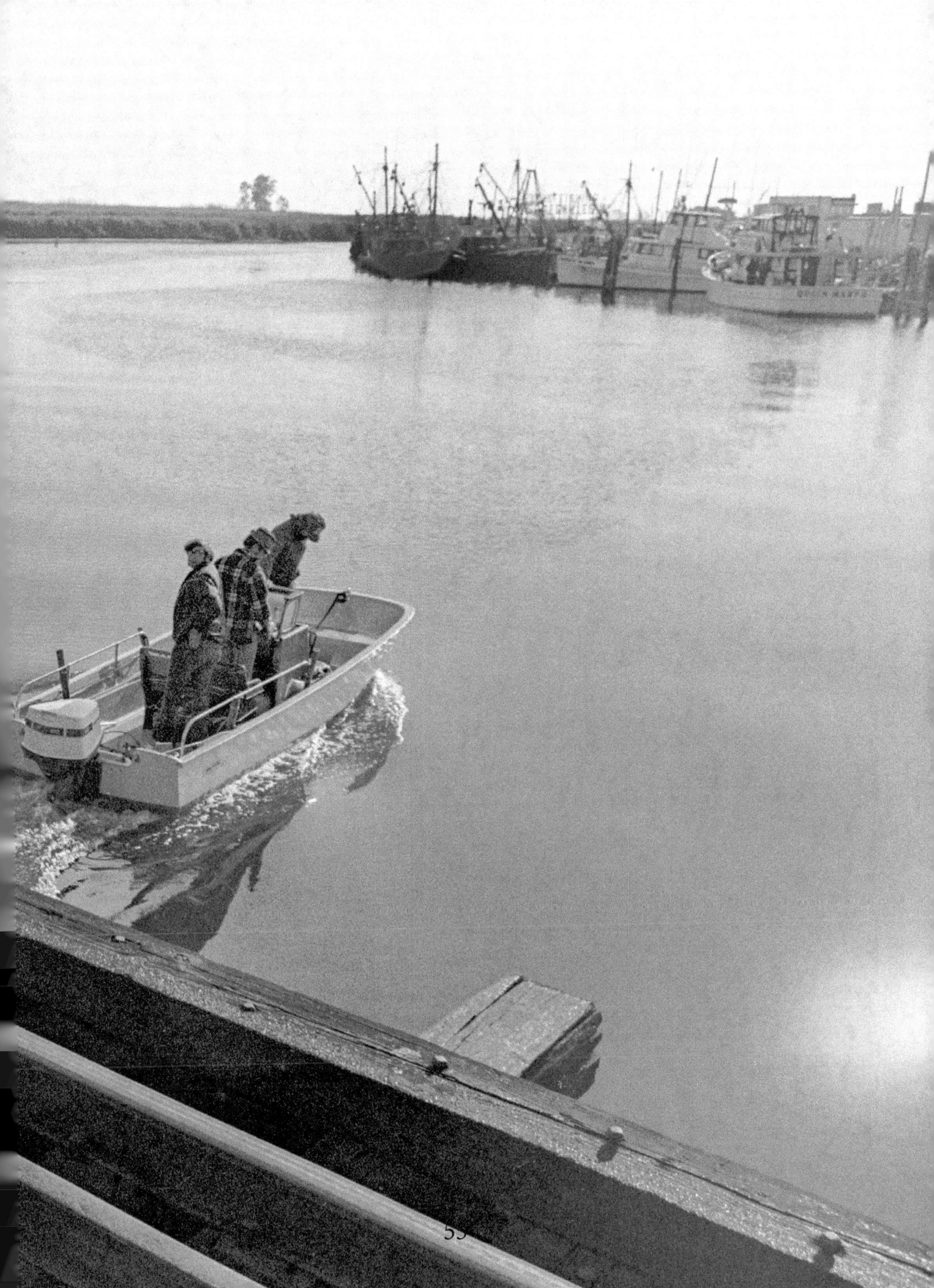

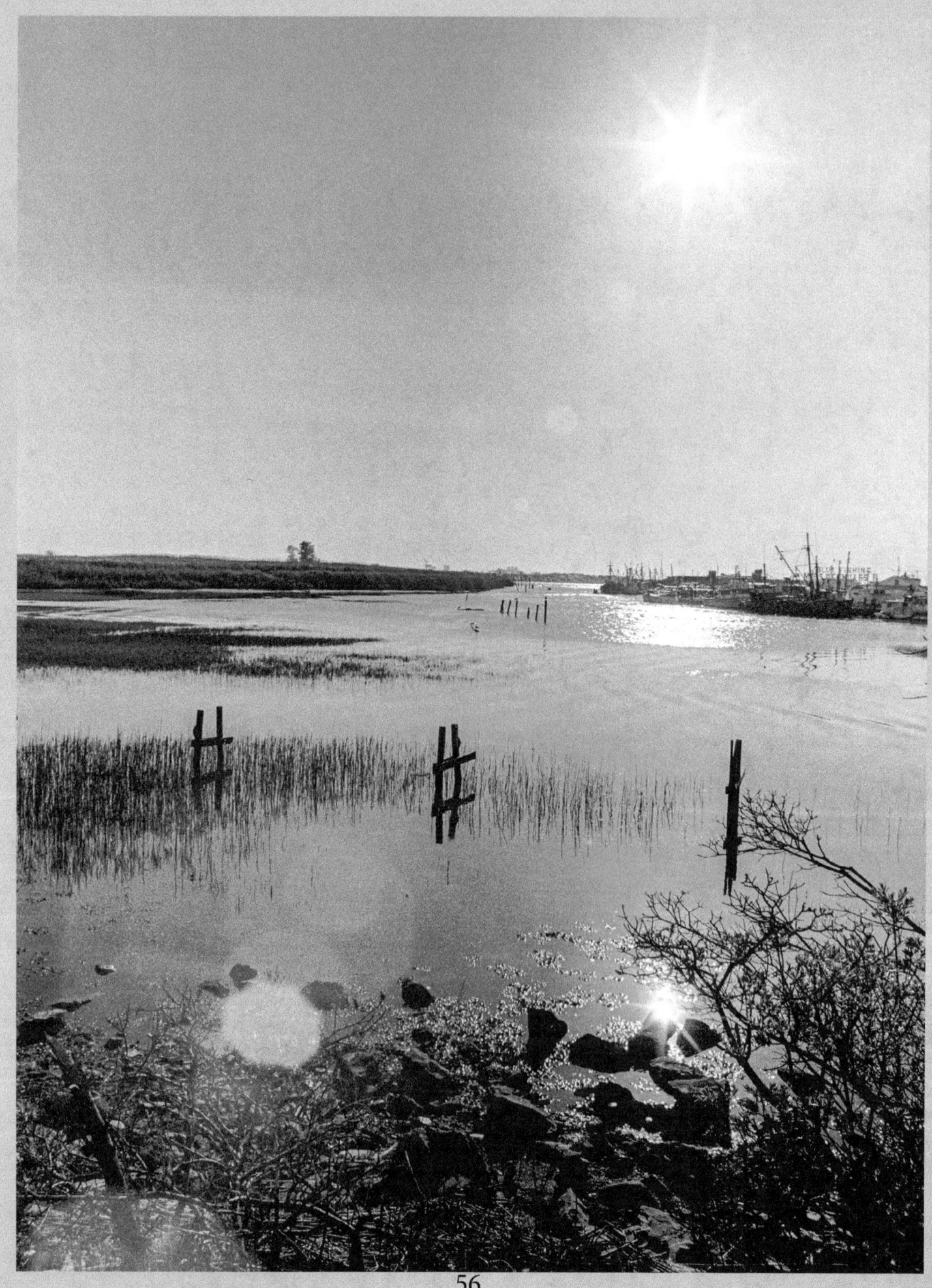